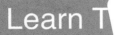 

MW01098090

Copyright © 2021 Geoff Jackson

Second publication July 2022

Learn Turkish In One Week

Chapters

1. <u>Adjectives</u>
2. <u>Airport</u>
3. <u>Animals</u>
4. <u>Bank</u>
5. <u>Beach</u>
6. <u>Buildings</u>
7. <u>Car</u>
8. <u>Clothes</u>
9. <u>Colours</u>
10. <u>Commands & Questions</u>
11. <u>Countries</u>
12. <u>Countryside</u>
13. <u>Days of the week</u>
14. <u>Descriptions</u>
15. <u>Directions</u>
16. <u>Doctor</u>
17. <u>Drinks</u>
18. <u>Emotions</u>
19. <u>Family</u>
20. <u>Farm</u>

Learn Turkish In One Week

21. Food

22. Fruits

23. General Conversation

24. Hobbies

25. Holidays

26. Hospital

27. Hotel

28. House

29. Market / Supermarket

30. Miscellaneous

31. Months

32. Numbers

33. Police

34. Pronouns

35. Restaurant

36. School

37. Time

38. Weather

39. Work

40. Vegetables

41. (Secret Bonus Page)

Learn Turkish In One Week

Turkish Pronunciation and Grammar

Turkey Introduction

Antalya

Alanya

Cappadocia

City of Ephesus

Dalyan

Fethiye

Göcek

Hisarönü

Istanbul

Marmaris

Pamukkale

Ölüdeniz

Learn Turkish In One Week

Turkish Pronunciation

The Turkish language is the 12th most spoken language in the world and Turkey has a fast developing economy which makes learning the Turkish language very important especially for individuals and companies wishing to do business in Turkey.

To learn Turkish we must first look at how each letter is pronounced and written so that we are able to read and speak new words.

letter is pronounced in Turkey except for ğ which has a little curved line above it. This letter is not pronounced but lengthens the preceding vowel slightly. Also each letter has only one sound.

a is short as in far.

ğ   is never pronounced.

ö "ur" as in burn

â   as in "latte"

It lengthens the.

p "puh" as in pencil

ay "eye" as in tight

preceding vowel.

There is no "q" in Turkish

b   "buh" as in bar

h   as in "happy"

r   "ruh" as in round

c   "juh" as in jam

ı   "uh" as in butter

s   "suh" as in send

ç   ch as in cheese

i   "ee" as in see

t   "tuh" as in table

d   "duh" as in day

j "s" as in measure

u "oo" as in oodles

e   "eh" as in get

k   "cuh" as in car

ü   "ew" in in few

ey "ay" as in day

l   "luh" as in lake

v "vuh" as in value

f   "fuh" as in face

m "muh" as in man

y "yuh" as in yes

Chapters

Learn Turkish In One Week

Turkish Grammar

The definite article (the)
In Turkish there is no separate word for the definite article (the).
dog = köpek   (kur peck)
the dog = köpek   (kur peck)

The word dog (köpek) can either mean "dog" or "the dog" in Turkish.
The indefinite article (a , an)
The indefinite article (a, an) is the same word for "one" (bir)
dog = köpek   (kur peck)
a dog = bir köpek   (bir kur peck)

Nouns

Nouns in Turkish do not have genders. There is no female or male association with any Turkish nouns.

Plural Nouns

To make a Turkish noun plural you have to add (ler) or (lar). Vowel harmony is used to decided which suffixes go on which word.

a, ı, o, u   = lar
e, i, ö, ü   = ler
cat = kedi   (keh dee)
cats = kediler   (keh dee ler)
bank = banka   (ban ka)
banks = bankalar   (ban ka lar)

More Pronunciation Tips

ey = "ay" as in may   o like oh in hot   z as in zebra

Learn Turkish In One Week

Suffixes

Turkish is a very special language in the fact that they use a lot of endings (suffixes) onto words to change the meaning of a word. In English we would simply use another word, but Turkish tend to use a lot of suffixes.

garden = bahçe   (ba cheh)

in the garden = bahçede (ba cheh day)

house = ev   (ev)

in the house = evde   (ev deh)

pool = havuz   (hav ooz)

in the pool = havuzda   (hav ooz da)

Adjectives

Turkish adjectives do not change and they always precede (go before) a noun that they are describing.

the slow car = yavaş araba   (ya vash a ra ba)

the beautiful flower = güzel çiçek   (gew zel chee chek)

the beautiful girl = güzel kız   (gew zel kuz)

If you put an adjective after a noun then the meaning changes.

the car is slow = araba yavaş   (a ra ba ya vash)

the girl is beautiful = kız güzel   (kuz gew zel)

Chapters

Learn Turkish In One Week

Adjectives

English	Turkish	Pronunciation
Tall	uzun	oo zoon
He is tall	o uzun	Oe oo zoon
Beautiful	güzel	gew zell
She is beautiful	o güzel	Oe gew zell
Soft	yumuşak	yoo moo shack
The pillow is soft	yastık yumuşak	yas tuck yoo moo shack
Dirty	kirli	keer lee
This plate is dirty	bu tabak kirli	boo ta bak keer lee
Happy	mutlu	mut loo
I am happy	mutluyum	mut loo yoom
Lonely	yalnız	yal nuz
My grandad is lonely	büyükbabam yalnız	bew yewk ba bam yal nuz
Tired	yorgun	yor goon
I'm tired	yorgunum	yor goon oom
Hungry	aç	ach
Are you hungry?	aç mısın	ach muh sun
Clean	temiz	teh meez
Is the table clean?	masa temiz mı	ma sa teh meez muh
Yes the table is clean	evet masa temiz	eh vet ma sa teh meez

Chapters

Learn Turkish In One Week

English	Turkish	Pronunciation
Easy	kolay	koh lie
Difficult	zor	zor
Angry	kızgın	kuz gun
Clever	akıllı	a cuh luh
Honest	dürüst	dur ruh st
Proud	gururlu	goo rur loo
Cold	soğuk	soe ook
Hot	sıcak	suh jak
Small	küçük	kew chewk
Very small	çok küçük	chok kew chewk
Cheap	ucuz	oo joo ss / (oo juice)
Expensive	pahalı	pa ha luh
Good	iyi	ee
Sad	üzgün	ewz gewn
Funny	komik	koh meek
Ugly	çirkin	cheer keen
Strong	güçlü	gewch lew (loo)
Near	yakın	ya kun
Low	düşük	dew shewk

Chapters

Learn Turkish In One Week

English	Turkish	Pronunciation
High	yüksek	yewk sek
Bad	kötü	kew tew
Scary	korkunç	kor coonch
Rich	zengin	zen geen
Poor	fakir	fak ir
Kind	nazik	nah zeeck
Interesting	ilginç	eel geench
Famous	ünlü	ewn lew (loo)
Calm	sakin	sah keen
Healthy	sağlıklı	saa luk luh
Sick	hasta	ha sta
New	yeni	yen nee
Old	eski	es kee
Big	büyük	bew yewk
Very big	çok büyük	chok bew yewk
Wide	geniş	geh neesh
Narrow	dar	dar
Quiet	sessiz	ses seez
Different	farklı	fark luh

Chapters

Learn Turkish In One Week

Airport

English	Turkish	Pronunciation
Airport	havalimanı	hava lee man uh
Airplane	uçak	oo chack
Customs	Gümrük	gewm rewk
Arrival	varış	va rush
Departure	kalkış	kal kush
Luggage	bagaj	ba garsh
Passenger	yolcu	yol joo
Passport	pasaport	pa sa port
Security Control	güvenlik kontrolü	gew ven leek con trol ew
Ticket	bilet	bee let
Stewardess	hostes	hoss tess
Hand luggage	el bagajı	el bag ah shyuh
Late	geç	gech
Terminal	terminal	ter mee nal
Cancel	iptal etmek	eep tal et mek
Currency exchange	döviz bürosu	dur veez bew oh soo
Luggage pickup	bagaj alma	bag arsh al ma
Plane ticket	uçak bileti	oo chack bee leh tee
Boarding	biniş	bee neesh

Chapters

Learn Turkish In One Week

English	Turkish	Pronunciation
Boarding gate	biniş kapısı	bee neesh ca puh suh
Name	isim	ee seem
Name	adı	a duh
Surname	soyadı	soy a duh
Nationality	milliyet	meel lee yet
Country	ülke	url keh
Language	dil	deel
Place of birth	doğum yeri	doh oom yeh ree
Date of birth	doğum tarihi	doh oom tah ree hee
I have a reservation	rezervasyonum var	rez er va see yon oom var
When does it land?	ne zaman iniyor	neh za man een ee yor
How do I get to the airport	havaalanına nasıl gidebilirim	hava alan un a na sull geed eh beel i reem
Gate	kapı	ka puh
Exit	çıkış	chuck ush
Entrance	giriş	gee reesh
Toilets	tuvaletler	too va let ler
Information	danışma	dan ush ma
Flight number	uçuş numarası	oo choosh noo ma ra suh
Boarding pass	binis kartı	been eesh car tuh

Chapters

Learn Turkish In One Week

Animals

English	Turkish	Pronunciation
Alligator	timsah	teem sa
Ant	karınca	ka run ja
Baboon	babun	ba boon
Bear	ayı	eye yuh
Butterfly	kelebek	kel eh beck
Beetle	böcek	bur jek
Bird	kuş	coosh
Cat	kedi	keh dee
Cheetah	çita	chee ta
Cockroach	hamamböceği	ha mam bur jeh ee
Cow	inek	een eck
Crab	yengeç	yen gech
Crocodile	timsah	teem sa
Caterpillar	tırtıl	tur tull
Chicken	tavuk	ta vook
Chimpanzee	şempanze	shem pan zeh
Donkey	eşek	esh eck
Deer	geyik	gay eek
Duck	ördek	ur deck

Chapters

Learn Turkish In One Week

English	Turkish	Pronunciation
Dog	köpek	kur peck
Dolphin	yunus	yoo noos
Eagle	kartal	car tal
Elephant	fil	feel
Fish	balık	ba luck
Fly	sinek	see neck
Fox	tilki	teel kee
Frog	kurbağa	kur baa
Goat	keçi	keh chee
Goose	kaz	kaz
Grasshopper	çekirge	chek eer geh
Giraffe	zürafa	zew ra fa
Gorilla	goril	gor eel
Hedgehog	kirpi	keer pee
Hippopotamus	suaygırı	soo eye guh ruh
Horse	at	at
Hyena	sırtlan	surt lan
Jellyfish	denizanası	den eez an a suh
Kangaroo	kanguru	kan goo roo

Chapters

Learn Turkish In One Week

English	Turkish	Pronunciation
Killer Whale	katil balina	ka teel ba leen a
Leopard	leopar	lay oh par
Lion	aslan	as lan
Lizard	kertenkele	ker ten kell eh
Lobster	ıstakoz	us ta coz
Monkey	maymun	meye moon
Meerkat	mirket	meer ket
Mouse	fare	far reh
Orangutan	orangutan	oh ran goo tan
Octopus	ahtapot	a ta pot
Ostrich	devekuşu	dev eh koo shoo
Otter	su samuru	soo sam oo roo
Panther	panter	pan ter
Peacock	tavuskuşu	tav oos koo shoo
Pelican	pelikan	peh lee can
Pigeon	güvercin	gew ver jeen
Polar Bear	kutup ayısı	coo toop ay uh suh
Parrot	papağan	pa pa an
Penguin	penguen	pen gwen

Chapters

Learn Turkish In One Week

English	Turkish	Pronunciation
Pig	domuz	doh mooz
Rabbit	tavşan	tav shan
Rat	sıçan	suh chan
Scorpion	akrep	a crep
Sea Lion	deniz aslanı	den eez as lan uh
Sea Horse	denizatı	den eez a tuh
Shark	köpekbalığı	kur peck ba luh
Shrimp	karides	car ee deh s
Salmon	somon	son mon
Sheep	koyun	koy oon
Skunk	kokarca	coh car ja
Snail	salyangoz	sal yan goz
Squid	kalamar	cal a mar
Swan	kuğu	coo oo
Sardine	sardalya	sar dal ya
Snake	yılan	yull an
Squirrel	sincap	seen jap
Tiger	kaplan	kap lan
Tortoise	tosbağa	toss ba aah

Chapters

Learn Turkish In One Week

English	Turkish	Pronunciation
Tuna	tonbalığı	ton ba luh
Turkey	hindi	heen dee
Wolf	kurt	kurt
Walrus	mors	mors
Wasp	yaban arısı	ya ban aah ruh suh
Zebra	zebra	zeh bra
The snail is slow	salyangoz yavaş	sal yan goz ya vash
A big elephant	büyük bir fil	bew yewk beer feel
The ant is small	karınca küçük	ka run ja kew chewk
Small ant	küçük karınca	kew chewk ka run ja
A very angry lion	çok kızgın bir aslan	chok kuz gun beer as lan
This monkey is happy	bu maymun mutlu	boo my moon moot loo
A tall giraffe	uzun bir zürafa	oo zoon beer zew ra fa
Black and white cow	siyah ve beyaz inek	see ya veh bay az een eck
This donkey is slow	bu eşek yavaş	boo esh eck ya vash
There is a snake	bir yılan var	beer yull an var
There's a shark	köpekbalığı var	kur peck ba luh var
Where's the dog?	köpek nerede	kur peck ner eh deh
Where's the cat?	kedi nerede	keh dee ner eh deh

Chapters

Learn Turkish In One Week

Turkey Introduction

Turkey is a beautiful country with stunning landscapes, warm, friendly people and a wonderful climate. It has a unique geographical position lying partly in Asia and partly in Europe.

The European portion of Turkey is very small comprising of about 3% of the country with the remaining 97% being in Asia. Throughout history it has acted as both a barrier and a bridge between these two continents. One of the most interesting facts about Istanbul is that it is a city divided by the Bosphorus River and two continents. The west bank lies on the European continent while the east bank is in Asia.

The English name of Turkey means "land of the Turks" and their official language is Turkish. Turkish is spoken in Turkey, Cyprus and other places in Europe and the Middle East.

There is roughly about 84 million people living in Turkey which is equivalent to about 1.1% of the total world population.

About 97-99% of the Turkish population is Muslim.

Santa Claus was born in Patara, Turkey. A holy man who people believed performed many miracles, including saving sailors from sinking ships. His tales of generosity became the basis for Santa Claus but he also became the patron saint of sailors.

Turkey exports about 75% of the worlds hazelnuts.

There are no deserts in Turkey and camels are not native to this country.

Chapters

Learn Turkish In One Week

Bank

English	Turkish	Pronunciation
Bank	banka	ban ka
Cash	nakit para	na keet pa ra
Money	para	pa ra
Balance	bakiye	ba kee yeh
Information desk	danışma	dan ush ma
Service charge	servis bedeli	ser vees bed el ee
Cash withdrawal	para çekmek	pa ra chek mek
Safe	kasa	ka sa
Bank account number	banka hesabı numarası	ban ka her sa buh noo ma ra suh
Debt	borç	borch
I would like to make a deposit	para yatırmak istiyorum	para ya tur mak ee stee yor oom
I would like to know my account balance	hesap bakiyemi bilmek istiyorum	her sap bak ee yemee beel mek istee yor oom
I would like to make a withdrawal	para çekmek istiyorum	pa ra check mek istee yor oom
I would like to transfer some money	biraz para transfer etmek istiyorum	beer az pa ra trans fer et mek ee stee yor oom
I need to pay a bill	bir fatura ödemem gerek	beer fa too ra ur deh mem geh rek
Where's the nearest bank	en yakın banka nerede	en ya kin ban ka ner ay deh
I forgot my password	şifremi unuttum	sheef remee oon oot toom

Chapters

Learn Turkish In One Week

Beach

English	Turkish	Pronunciation
Sea	deniz	den eez
Beach	plaj	pee larsh
Sandy beach	kumlu plaj	coom loo pee larsh
Ocean	okyanus	ock yan oos
Sun	güneş	gewn esh
Sunny	güneşli	gewn esh lee
Midday sun	öğle güneşi	ur leh gewn esh ee
Swim	yüzmek	yewz mek
Swimming	yüzme	yewz may
He is swimming	o yüzüyor	oe yewz ee yor
She is swimming	o yüzüyor	oe yewz ee yor
I want to swim	ben yüzmek istiyorum	ben yewz mek ee stee yor oom
Towel	havlu	hav loo
Beach towel	plaj havlusu	pee larsh hav loo soo
Sand	kum	koom
Sand castle	kumdan kale	koom dan ka leh
The sand is hot	kum sıcak	koom suh jak
Shell	kabuk	ka book

Chapters

Learn Turkish In One Week

English	Turkish	Pronunciation
Seashell	deniz kabuğu	den eez ka boo oo
Swimsuit	mayo	meye oe
The water is cold	su soğuk	soo soh ook
The sea is warm	deniz sıcak	den eez suh jak
It's too hot	çok sıcak	chok suh jak
I want a drink	ben bir içecek istiyorum	ben ber eech eh jek ees tee yor oom
Bikini	bikini	bee kee nee
Sunscreen	güneş kremi	gewn esh crem ee
Sunglasses	güneş gözlüğü	gwen esh gurz lew oo
These sunglasses are new	bu güneş gözlüğü yeni	boo gewn esh gurz loo oo yen ee
Sea urchin	deniz kestanesi	den eez keh stan eh see
Palm tree	palmiye	pal mee yeh
Sunbed	şezlong	shez long
How much are the sunbeds	şezlong ne kadar	shez long neh ka dar
Lifeguard	cankurtaran	jan kur ta ran
Help	yardım edin	yar dum ed een
Can you help me	bana yardım edebilir misin	ba na yar dum ed eh beel ir mee seen
Please help me	lütfen bana yardım edin	loot fen ban a yar dum ed een

Chapters

Learn Turkish In One Week

English	Turkish	Pronunciation
Umbrella	şemsiye	shem see yeh
The shore	sahil	sar heel
Crab / the crab	yengeç / yengeç	yen gech / yen gech
The fish	balık	ba luk
Shark	köpekbalığı	kur pek ba luh
Look shark	bak köpekbalığı	bak kur pek ba luh
Hot	sıcak	suh jak
It is very hot	çok sıcak	chok suh jak
Wave	dalga	dal ga
Starfish	deniz yıldızı	den eez yul duz uh
Hat	şapka	shap ka
Where's my hat	şapkam nerede	shap kam ner eh deh
My hat	şapkam	shap kam
Summer	yaz	yaz
Sunburn	güneş yanığı	gewn esh yan uh
To dive	dalmak	dal mak
To surf	sörf yapmak	surf yap mak
Holiday	tatil	ta teel
The beach is crowded	plaj kalabalık	pee larsh ka la ba luk

Chapters

Learn Turkish In One Week

English	Turkish	Pronunciation
Sunset	gün batımı	gewn bat uh muh
Bucket	kova	koh va
Shovel	kürek	kew rek
Surfboard	sörf tahtası	surf ta ta suh
Beach umbrella	plaj şemsiyesi	pee larsh shem see yay see
Beach bag	plaj çantası	pee larsh chan ta suh
Bucket and spade	kova ve kürek	ko va vay kew rek
Life jacket	can yeleği	jan yeh leh ee
Snorkel	şnorkel	shuh nor kell
Sunbathing	güneşlenme	gewn esh len meh
Mountain	dağ	daa
Tree	ağaç	aach
Turtle	kaplumbağa	ka ploom baa a
Flippers	paletler	pa let ler
Sun protection	güneş koruması	gewn esh kor oom a suh
Coast guard	sahil güvenlik	sar heel gew ven leek
On the beach	sahilde	sar heel deh
Windy	rüzgarlı	rewz gar luh
He's in the water	o suda	oe soo da

Chapters

Learn Turkish In One Week

Buildings

English	Turkish	Pronunciation
Shopping centre	alışveriş Merkezi	a lush vereesh mer kez ee
Bank	banka	ban ka
Bar	bar	bar
Town hall	belediye binası	bel eh dee yeh been a suh
Petrol station	benzin istasyonu	ben zeen eestas yon oo
Mosque	cami	jam ee
Information office	danışma bürosu	dan ush ma bew roh soo
Pharmacy	eczane	ehj zar neh
Factory	fabrika	fa bree ka
Bakery	fırın	fuh run
Fair	fuar	foo ar
Garage	garaj	ga rarsh
Night club	gece kulübü	geh jeh koo lew buh
Optician	gözlükçü	gurz lewk chew
Turkish bath	hamam	ha mam
Prison	hapishane	ha pee sar neh
Hospital	hastane	has tan neh
Airport	havalimanı	hav a lee man uh
Zoo	hayvanat bahçesi	heye van at bach eh see

Chapters

Learn Turkish In One Week

English	Turkish	Pronunciation
Police station	karakol	kar a coll
Cathedral	katedral	cat ed ral
Church	kilise	kee lee seh
Bookstore	kitabevi	kee tab ev ee
Bridge	köprü	kur proo
Hairdresser's	kuaför	kuh a fur
Casino	kumarhane	cuh mar har neh
Library	kütüphane	kew tewp har neh
Restaurant	lokanta	Loh can ta
Cemetery	mezarlık	mez ar luk
Museum	müze	mew zay
School	okul	oh cool
Bus terminal	otobüs terminali	otoe bews ter meen a lee
Car park	otopark	otoe park
Toll road	paralı yol	pa ra luh yol
Post office	postane	pos ta neh
Palace	saray	sa reye
Cinema	sinema	seen eh ma
Taxi stop	taksi durağı	tak see doo rar uh

Chapters

Learn Turkish In One Week

English	Turkish	Pronunciation
Theatre	tiyatro	tee ya troe
Train station	tren istasyonu	tren ee stas yon oo
Tunnel	tünel	tewn el
University	üniversite	ewn ee ver see teh
Swimming pool	yüzme havuzu	yewz meh hav oo zoo
Castle	kale	ka leh
Castle / Chateau	şato	sha toe
Supermarket	süpermarket	soo per mar ket
Farm	çiftlik	cheeft leek
Farm house	çiftlik evi	cheeft leek ev ee
House	ev	ev
Hotel	otel	oe tell
Gymnasium	spor salonu	spor sal on oo
Lighthouse	deniz feneri	den eez fen er ee
Market	market	mar ket
Market	pazar	pa zar
Office	ofis	oh fee s
Pyramid	piramit	pee ra meet
Skyscraper	gökdelen	gurk deh len

Chapters

Learn Turkish In One Week

Antalya

Antalya is located on the southwest coast, bordered by the impressive Taurus Mountains. It is the largest Turkish city on the Mediterranean coast outside the aegean region with over one million people.

Antalya is Turkey's biggest international sea resort, located on the Turkish Riviera. Tourism plays an important part to this region with over 13 million tourists passing through the city in 2019.

The best time to visit Antalya is between April and October as the weather is pleasant throughout the day, however in July and August it can get extremely hot, especially during the day.

Chapters

Learn Turkish In One Week

Antalya is a fabulous place to visit with wonderful beaches, traditional Turkish culture, Aqua Land, Dolphin Land, a much more.

Take a scary cable car ride and view this magnificent city from up high or visit the old town centre which is buzzing with bars, restaurants and clubs.

There's historical monuments and a vibrant modern nightlife and breathtaking waterfalls that will leave you speechless.

You'll find mosques, churches, madrasahs, hammams, museums and even Hadrian's Gate which was erected in honour of the AD 130 visit by Emperor Hadrian himself.

An impressive Roman Theatre commonly thought to be the best preserved in the world can be found 47 kilometres east in Aspendos.

Chapters

Learn Turkish In One Week

Car

English	Turkish	Pronunciation
Where can I park the car?	arabayı nereye park edebilirim	a ra ba yuh ner reh yeh park ed eh beel ir eem
Can I park here?	buraya park edebilir miyim	boo ra ya park ed eh beel ir meem
Where's the nearest car park?	en yakın otopark nerede	en ya kun oh toe park ner eh deh
Where's the nearest petrol station?	en yakın benzin istasyonu nerede	en ya kun ben zeen ee stas yon oo neh reh deh
Fill it up please	doldurun lütfen	dol doo roon lewt fen
Check the oil please	yağı kontrol edin lütfen	yaa uh con trol eh deen lewt fen
This tyre is flat	bu lastik patlak	boo las teek pat lak
There's been an accident	bir kaza oldu	beer ka za ol doo
May I use your phone	telefonunuzu kullanabilir miyim	tel eh fon oon oo zoo kool an a beel ir meem
Please call a doctor	doktor çağırın lütfen	dok tor cha uh run lewt fen
Please call an ambulance	ambulans çağırın lütfen	am boo lans cha uh run lewt fen
Is your car insured?	arabanız sigortalı mı	a ra ban uz see gor ta luh muh
My car is insured	arabam sigortalı	a ra bam see gor ta luh
My car has broken down	arabam bozuldu	a ra bam boz ool doo
What's wrong with it?	nesi var	neh see var
The radiator is leaking	radyatör sızdırıyor	rad ya tur suz duh ruh yor

Chapters

Learn Turkish In One Week

English	Turkish	Pronunciation
Axle	aks	aks
Battery	akü	a kew
Shock absorber	amortisör	a mor tee sur
Aerial	anten	an ten
Car	araba	a ra ba
My car	arabam	a ra bam
Your car is fast	araban hızlı	a ra ban huz luh
My car is too small	arabam çok küçük	a ra bam chok kew chewk
What colour is your car?	araban ne renk	a ra ban neh renk
My car is white	arabam beyaz	a ra bam bay az
Window	pencere	pen jeh reh
Rear window	arkacam	ar ka jam
Trunk / boot	bagaj	bag arsh
Petrol	benzin	ben zeen
Petrol pump	benzin pompası	ben zeen pomp a suh
Car parts	araba parçaları	a ra ba par chal a ruh
Mudguard	çamurluk	cham oor look
Clutch	debriyaj	deh bree yarsh
Clutch pedal	debriyaj pedalı	deh bree yarsh ped a luh

Chapters

Learn Turkish In One Week

English	Turkish	Pronunciation
Mirror	ayna	eye na
Rear mirror	dikiz aynası	dee keez eye na suh
Steering column	direksiyon mili	dee rek see yon mee lee
Distributor	distribütör	dees tree bew tur
Steering wheel	direksiyon	dee rek see yon
Exhaust	egzoz	eg zoz
Exhaust pipe	egzoz borusu	eg zoz bor oo soo
Camshaft	eksantrik mili	eck san treek mee lee
Seat belt / safety belt	emniyet kemeri	em nee yet kem eh ree
Headlight	far	far
Headlights	farlar	far lar
Filter	filtre	feel treh
Brake	fren	fren
Brake drum	fren kampanası	fren cam pan a suh
Brake shoes	fren pabuçları	fren pa booch la ruh
Air filter	hava filtresi	ha va feel treh see
Spark plug	buji	boo shyee
Cable	kablo	cab loe
Bonnet	kaput	ka poot

Chapters

Learn Turkish In One Week

English	Turkish	Pronunciation
Open the bonnet	kaputu aç	ka poo too ach
Close the bonnet	kaputu kapat	ka poo too ka pat
Carburettor	karbüratör	car bew ra tur
Ignition	kontak	kon tak
Ignition key	kontak anahtarı	kon tak an a ta ruh
Crankshaft	krank mili	crank mee lee
Wheel	tekerlek	teh ker lek
Tire	lastik	las teek
Starter motor	marş motoru	marsh moh toh roo
Engine	motor	moh tor
Windscreen	öncam	urn jam
Piston	piston	pee ston
Licence plate	plaka	pla ka
Radiator	radyatör	rad ya tur
Piston rings	segmanlar	seg man lar
Cylinder	silindir	see leen dir
Suspension	süspansiyon	sew span see yon
Bumper	tampon	tam pon
Thermostat	termostat	ter moe stat

Chapters

Learn Turkish In One Week

English	Turkish	Pronunciation
Oil filter	yağ filtresi	yar feel treh see
Minimum speed	asgari sürat	as ga ree sew rat
Maximum speed	azami sürat	az a mee sew rat
Two way traffic	çift yönlü yol	cheeft yurn lew yol
Road signs	yol işaretleri	yol ee shar et leh ree
Motorway	otoban	oh toe ban
No parking	park yapılmaz	park ya pul maz
Parking	park yeri	park yeh ree
No overtaking	sollamak yasaktır	sol la mak yas ak tur
One way street	tek yönlü yol	tek yurn lew yol
One way traffic	tek yönlü trafik	tek yurn lew tra feek
I have a new car	yeni bir arabam var	yen ee bir a ra bam var
Where is it?	nerede	neh reh deh
Outside	dışarıda	dush a ruh da
In the garage	garajda	ga rarsh da
This is my car	bu benim arabam	boo ben eem a ra bam
My new car is blue	yeni arabam mavi	yen ee a ra bam mar vee
My old car was too slow	eski arabam çok yavaştı	es kee a ra bam chok ya vash tuh
Where shall we go?	nereye gidelim	neh reh yeh geed eh leem

Chapters

Learn Turkish In One Week

Clothes

English	Turkish	Pronunciation
Anorak	anorak	an or ack
Shoes	ayakkabı	eye ack ka buh
Jacket	ceket	jeh ket
Boots	çizme	cheez meh
Socks	çorap	chor ap
Tracksuit	eşofman	esh off man
Clothing	giyim	gee yeem
Shirt	gömlek	gurm lek
Cardigan	hırka	hur ka
Underwear	iç çamaşırı	eech char ma shuh ruh
Pullover / sweater	kazak	kaz ak
Tie	kravat	cra vat
Underpants	külot	kew lot
Overcoat	palto	pal toe
Trousers	pantolon	pan toh lon
Bow tie	papyon	pap yon
Pyjamas	pijama	pee shya ma
Tuxedo	smokin	smoe keen
Sports shoes	spor ayakkabı	spor eye ak ka buh

Chapters

Learn Turkish In One Week

English	Turkish	Pronunciation
Shorts	şort	short
Suit	takım elbise	ta kum ayl bee seh
Slippers	terlik	ter leek
Belt	kemer	keh mer
T-shirt	tişört	tee shurt
Raincoat	yağmurluk	ya moor look
Waistcoat	yelek	yeh lek
Bikini	bikini	bee kee nee
Blouse	bluz	blooz
Bathrobe	bornoz	bor noz
Stockings	çorap	chor ap
Leather dress	deri elbise	deh ree el bee seh
Dress	elbise	el bee seh
Leather suit	deri takım	deh ree ta kum
Skirt	etek	et eck
Nightdress	gecelik	geh jeh leek
Wedding gown	gelinlik	geh leen leek
Panties	külot	Kur lot
Tights	külotlu çorap	kur lot loo chor ap

Chapters

Learn Turkish In One Week

English	Turkish	Pronunciation
Coat	manto	man toe
Fur coat	kürk manto	kurk man toe
Swimsuit	mayo	meye oe
Bra	sutyen	soot yen
Summer dress	yazlık elbise	yaz luck el bee seh
How much is this shirt	bu gömlek ne kadar	boo gurm lek neh ka dar
The black shirt	siyah gömlek	see ya gurm lek
Leather	deri	deh ree
Silk	ipek	ee pek
Velvet	kadife	ka dee feh
Linen	keten	keh ten
Sheepskin	koyun postu	koy oon pos too
Corduroy	fitilli kadife	fee teel lee kad ee feh
Material	malzeme	mal zeh meh
Nylon	naylon	neye lon
Cotton	pamuk	pa mook
Suede	süet	soo et
Wool	yün	yewn
Striped	çizgili	cheez gee lee

Chapters

Learn Turkish In One Week

English	Turkish	Pronunciation
Tight	dar	dar
Tight	sıkı	suh cuh
This shirt is too tight	bu gömlek çok sıkı	boo gurm lek chok suh cuh
Plain	sade	sar deh
Plain	düz	dooz
Patterned	desenli	deh sen lee
Loose	bol	bol
Loose	gevşek	gev shek
This dress is too loose	bu elbise çok gevşek	boo el bee seh chok gev shek
Thin	ince	een jeh
Thick	kalın	ka lun
Short	kısa	ku sa
Long	uzun	oo zoon
Lace	dantel	dan tel
Button	düğme	dew meh
Button	buton	boo ton
Pocket	cep	jep
Width	en	en
Zipper	fermuar	fer moo ar

Chapters

Learn Turkish In One Week

English	Turkish	Pronunciation
Inside pocket	iç cep	eech jep
Button hole	ilik	eel eek
Short sleeved	kısa kollu	cuh sa kol loo
Lapel	klapa	cla pa
Braces	pantolon askısı	pan ta lon ask uh suh
Long sleeved	uzun kollu	oo zoon kol loo
Collar	yaka	ya ka
Headscarf	başörtüsü	ba shur tew soo
Braclet	bilezik	bee leh zeek
Wallet	cüzdan	jewz dan
Purse	çanta	chan ta
Bag	çanta	chan ta
Lighter	çakmak	chak mak
Handbag	el çantası	el chan ta suh
Gloves	eldiven	el dee ven
Scarf	eşarp	eh sharp
Glasses	gözlük	gurz lewk
Sunglasses	güneş gözlüğü	gewn esh gurz lew oo
Scarf	kaşkol	cash kol

Chapters

Learn Turkish In One Week

English	Turkish	Pronunciation
Necklace	kolye	kol yeh
Tie clip	kravat iğnesi	cra vat ee neh see
Earrings	küpe	kew peh
Handkerchief	mendil	man deel
Jewllery	mücevherat	mew jev heh rat
Pendant	pandantif	pan dan teef
Hairpin	saç tokası	sach tok a suh
Shawl	şal	shall
Hat	şapka	shap ka
Umbrella	şemsiye	shem see yeh
Comb	tarak	ta rak
Turban	türban	tur ban
Ring	yüzük	yew zewk
Chain	zincir	zeen jeer
Where's my hat	şapkam nerede	shap kam neh reh deh
My bag is big	çantam büyük	chan tam bew yewk
The dress is beautiful	elbise güzel	el bee seh gew zell
My pants are tight	pantolonum sıkı	pan ta lon oom suh kuh
How much is this dress?	bu elbise ne kadar	boo el bee seh neh ka dar

Chapters

Learn Turkish In One Week

Colours

English	Turkish	Pronunciation
Red	kırmızı	kur muh zuh
Pink	pembe	pem beh
Orange	turuncu	tuh run joo
Yellow	sarı	sa ruh
Green	yeşil	yeh sheel
Blue	mavi	mar vee
Light blue	açık mavi	a chuck mar vee
Dark blue	koyu mavi	koy oo mar vee
Purple	mor	mor
Turquoise	turkuaz	turk koo az
Brown	kahverengi	ka ver ren gee
Black	siyah	see ya
White	beyaz	bay az
Grey	gri	gree
A red apple	bir kırmızı elma	beer kur muh zuh el ma
The apple is red	elma kırmızı	el ma kur muh zuh
White door	beyaz kapı	bay az ka puh
The door is white	kapı beyaz	ka puh bay az
The carpet is brown	halı kahverengi	ha luh ka ver ren gee

Chapters

Learn Turkish In One Week

Alanya

Alanya is about 72 miles from Antalya, straight along the stunning coastline. It's a busy town with three beaches and plenty of hotels, bars and shops.

It is said that in 44 BC the very much in love Roman general, Mark Antony, gave this entire region to the love of his life, Cleopatra.

As you approach the town you can't help but notice the medieval castle perched on a rocky peninsula jutting out into the Mediterranean Sea, 250 metres above the town, keeping a watchful eye on the the people below. The wall which surrounds the castle is 4 miles long with 140 towers for protection.

The defenders of the castle were able to survive prolonged sieges due to the 400 cisterns that were built for drinking water. These are hidden in the area.

There is plenty to do in Alanya from lazy days on one of the beautiful beaches, water sports for the more energetic and an abundance of restaurants, bars and souvenir shops.

You could also visit the ancient city of Laertes which is located in Mahmutlar. This is in the neighbourhood of Gözüküçüklü (small eyed people area).

Another place well worth a visit is Sapadere Canyon which has awesome waterfalls, crystal clear waters and amazing walks.

Alanya is overlooked by magnificent Taurus mountains making this beautiful Turkish town well worth a visit.

Chapters

Learn Turkish In One Week

Commands & Questions

English	Turkish	Pronunciation
What	ne	neh
Where	nerede	neh reh deh
Why	neden	neh den
When	ne zaman	neh za man
Who	kim	keem
Whose	kimin	keem een
To whom	kime	keem eh
Which	hangi	han gee
How	nasıl	na sull
How old	kaç yaşında	kach ya shun da
How many	kaç tane	kach tar neh
How much	ne kadar	neh ka dar
How much	kaç para	kach para
What time is it	saat kaç	sart kach
How far	ne kadar uzak	Neh ka dar oo zak
How far is it to	ne kadar uzaklıkta	neh ka dar oo zak luk ta
How often	ne kadar sık	neh ka dar suk
How long for	ne kadar süre için	neh ka dar sew reh eech een
What happened	ne oldu	neh ol doo

Chapters

Learn Turkish In One Week

English	Turkish	Pronunciation
What do you want	ne istiyorsun	neh ee stee yor soon
What would you like	ne istersin	neh ee ster seen
What would you like to do	ne yapmak istersiniz	neh yap mak ee ster seen eez
What would you like to eat	ne yemek istersiniz	neh yeh mek ee ster seen eez
What would you like to drink	ne içmek istersiniz	neh eech meck ee ster seen iz
What would you like to do today	bugün ne yapmak istersin iz	boo goon neh yap mak ee ster seen eez
What is your name	adınız ne	ad un uz neh
What is your surname	soyadınız ne	soy a dun uz neh
Were are you from	nerelisin	neh reh lee seen
Where do you live	nerede yaşıyorsun	ne reh deh ya shuh yor soon
What are you looking for	ne arıyorsunuz	neh a ruh yor soon ooz
What did you say	ne dediniz	neh ded een eez
What did you see	ne gördünüz	neh gur dewn ooz
Who's that	şu kim	shoo keem
Who's is this	bu kimin	boo keem een
Where is	nerede	neh reh deh
Where's the nearest	en yakın … nerede	en ya cun neh reh deh
Where's the nearest bank	en yakın banka nerede	en ya cun ban ka neh reh deh
Where are we	neredeyiz	ne reh deh yeez

Chapters

Learn Turkish In One Week

English	Turkish	Pronunciation
Where can I buy	nereden … alabilirim	Neh reh den al a beel ir eem
Where can I buy milk	nereden süt alabilirim	neh reh den sewt al a beel ir eem
Where are you going	nereye gidiyorsun	neh reh yeh geed ee yor soon
Where are you going now	şimdi nereye gidiyorsun	sheem dee neh reh yeh geed ee yor soon
Where are you going today	bugün nereye gidiyorsun	boo gewn neh reh yeh geed ee yor soon
How much do you want	ne kadar istiyorsunuz	neh ka dar ees tee yor soon ooz
Is this yours	bu sizin mi	boo seez een mee
Can I sit here	buraya oturabilir miyim	boo ra ya oh tur a beel ir meem
Look at that	şuna bak	shoon a bak
Please hurry up	acele et lütfen	a jell eh et lewt fen
Come here	buraya gel	boo ra ya gel
Look	bak	bak
Come	gel	gel
Go	git	geet
Please come	lütfen gel	lewt fen gel
Please go	lütfen git	lewt fen geet
Please look	lütfen bak	lewt fen bak
Please read	lütfen oku	lewt fen oh coo

Chapters

Learn Turkish In One Week

English	Turkish	Pronunciation
Please don't run	lütfen koşma	lewt fen kosh ma
Run	koş	kosh
Please don't tell	lütfen söyleme	lewt fen soy leh meh
Come in please	içeri gir lütfen	ee cherry gir lewt fen
Sit down	otur	oe toor
Stand up	kalk	kalk
Stand up	ayağa kalk	eye a kalk
Eat	ye	yeh
Call me	ara beni	a ra ben ee
Swim	yüz	yewz
Tell	söyle	soy leh
Take	al	al
Take a pen	kalem al	ka lem al
Read a book	kitap oku	kee tap oh coo
Speak	konuş	con oosh
Speak Turkish	Türkçe konuş	turk chey con oosh
Speak English please	lütfen ingilizce konuş	lewt fen een geel eez jeh con oosh
Don't run	koşma	kosh ma
Don't do that please	yapma lütfen	yap ma lewt fen

Chapters

Learn Turkish In One Week

English	Turkish	Pronunciation
Don't go	gitme	geet meh
Please don't go	lütfen gitme	lewt fen geet meh
Please don't run	lütfen koşma	lewt fen kosh ma
Stop	dur	doo r
Drink	iç	eech
Listen	dinle	deen leh
Understand	anla	an la
Sleep	uyu	oo yoo
Clap	alkışla	al kush la
Smile	gül	gewl
Cry	ağla	ar la
Talk to me	benimle konuş	ben eem leh con oosh
Call me tomorrow	beni yarın ara	ben ee yar un a ra
Write	yaz	yaz
Eat with me	benimle ye	ben eem leh yeh
Drink with me	benimle iç	ben eem leh eech
Don't come	gelme	gel meh
Don't speak	konuşma	con oosh ma
Don't speak English	ingilizce konuşma	een geel eez jeh con oosh ma

Chapters

Learn Turkish In One Week

English	Turkish	Pronunciation
Don't listen	dinleme	deen leh meh
Don't look	bakma	bak ma
Don't eat	yeme	yeh meh
Don't drink	içme	eech meh
Don't sleep	uyuma	oo yoo ma
Walk	yürü	yew roo
Don't walk	yürüme	yew roo meh
Open	aç	ach
Open the door	kapıyı aç	cap uh yuh ach
Don't open	açma	ach ma
Don't open the door	kapıyı açma	ka puh yuh ach ma
Speak slowly	yavaş konuş	ya vash kon oosh
Speak slowly please	yavaş konuş lütfen	ya vash kon oosh lewt fen
Don't cry	ağlama	ar la ma
Don't stop	durma	doo r ma
Don't stand up	kalkma	kalk ma
Don't stand up	ayağa kalkma	eye a kalk ma
Don't talk to me	benimle konuşma	ben eem leh kon oosh ma
Don't call me tomorrow	beni yarın arama	ben ee ya run a ra ma

Chapters

Learn Turkish In One Week

Countries

English	Turkish	Pronunciation
Argentina	Arjantin	ar shyan teen
Australia	Avustralya	a voo stral ya
Austria	Avusturya	a voo stur ya
Belgium	Belçika	bel chee ka
Brazil	Brezilya	breh zeel ya
Bulgaria	Bulgaristan	bool gar ee stan
Cambodia	Kamboçya	cam boh chya
Canada	Kanada	ka na da
China	Çin	cheen
Colombia	Kolombiya	kol om bee ya
Cyprus	Kıbrıs	kuh brus
Denmark	Danimarka	dan ee mar ka
Egypt	Mısır	muh sur
Finland	Finlandiya	feen lan dee ya
France	Fransa	fran sa
Germany	Almanya	al man ya
Greece	Yunanistan	yoo nan ee stan
Hungary	Macaristan	ma jar ee stan
Iceland	İzlanda	eez lan da

Chapters

Learn Turkish In One Week

English	Turkish	Pronunciation
India	Hindistan	heen dee stan
Indonesia	Endonezya	en doe nez ya
Iran	İran	ee ran
Iraq	Irak	ur rack
Ireland	İrlanda	eer lan da
Israel	İsrail	ees rar eel
Italy	İtalya	ee tal ya
Jamaica	Jamaika	shya ma ee ka
Japan	Japonya	shya pon ya
Lebanon	Lübnan	lewb nan
Libya	Libya	leeb ya
Malaysia	Malezya	ma leh zee ya
Maldives	Maldivler	mal deev ler
Malta	Malta	mal ta
Mexico	Meksika	mek see ka
Morocco	Fas	fas
Netherlands	Hollanda	ho lan da
New Zealand	Yeni Zelanda	yeh nee zeh lan da
North Korea	Kuzey Kore	koo zay kor eh

Chapters

Learn Turkish In One Week

English	Turkish	Pronunciation
South Korea	Güney Kore	goo nay cor eh
Norway	Norveç	nor vech
Pakistan	Pakistan	pah kee stan
Philippines	Filipinler	fee lee peen ler
Poland	Polonya	pol on ya
Portugal	Portekiz	por teh keez
Romania	Romanya	roh man ya
Russia	Rusya	roo s ya
Saudi Arabia	Suudi Arabistan	soo dee a rab ee stan
South Africa	Güney Afrika	gew nay af ree ca
Spain	ispanya	ee span ya
Sweden	İsveç	ees vech
Switzerland	İsviçre	ees veech reh
Syria	Suriye	soo ree yeh
Thailand	Tayland	teye land
Tunisia	Tunus	too noos
Turkey	Türkiye	tur kee yeh
United Kingdom	Birleşik Krallık	beer leh sheek cral luck
United States of America	Amerika Birleşik Devletleri	ameh ree ca beer leh sheek dev let leh ree

Chapters

Learn Turkish In One Week

Countryside

English	Turkish	Pronunciation
Tree	ağaç	aaach
Grass	çim	cheem
River	nehir	neh heer
Flowers	çiçekler	chee chek ler
Hedge	çit	cheet
Mountain	dağ	dar
Gate	kapı	ka puh
Countryside	kırsal bölge	kur sal burl geh
Cave	mağara	mar ra
Waterfall	şelale	shell a leh
Hill	tepe	teh peh
Village	köy	koy
Fence	çit	cheet
Goats	keçiler	keh chee ler
Snakes	yılanlar	yul an lar
Lake	göl	gurl
Fish	balık	ba luk
Bee	bal arısı	bal a ruh suh
Wasp	yaban arısı	ya ban a ruh suh

Chapters

Cappadocia

Another hidden gem is Cappadocia in central Turkey. It is known for it's cone-shaped rock formations, huddled together in Monks Valley, Göreme and other local areas. An underground city was carved into the rock by cave dwellers many years ago where their homes were very cool and protective from the blistering sun outside. The landscape is like a picture book and a visit to Cappadocia isn't complete until you've woken before the sun to watch hundreds of hot air balloons sailing majestically, through the sky. Absolutely breathtaking! A stay in one of these hotels carved from rock, along with a hot air balloon ride, is an experience not to be missed.

Chapters

Learn Turkish In One Week

Days of the week

English	Turkish	Pronunciation
Monday	Pazartesi	pa zar teh see
Tuesday	Salı	sa luh
Wednesday	Çarşamba	char sham ba
Thursday	Perşembe	per shem beh
Friday	Cuma	joo ma
Saturday	Cumartesi	joo mar teh see
Sunday	Pazar	paz ar
This Saturday	Bu Cumartesi	boo joo mar teh see
Next Wednesday	gelecek çarşamba	geh leh jek char sham ba
Week	hafta	haf ta
Next week	gelecek hafta	geh leh jek haf ta
In one week	bir hafta içinde	bir haf ta eech in deh
Weekend	hafta sonu	haf ta son oo
This weekend	bu hafta sonu	boo haf ta son oo
Yesterday	dün	dewn
Tomorrow	yarın	ya run
Morning	sabah	sa ba
Tomorrow morning	yarın sabah	ya run sa ba
See you tomorrow morning	yarın sabah görüşürüz	ya run sa ba gur rew shew rooz

Chapters

Learn Turkish In One Week

Descriptions

English	Turkish	Pronunciation
Body	vücut	vew joot
Fat	şişman	sheesh man
Skinny / Scrawny	cılız	jull uz
Skinny	sıska	sus ka
Thin	ince	een jeh
Tall	uzun boylu	ooz oon boy loo
Small	küçük	kew chewk
Short	kısa	kuh sa
Slim	narin	na reen
Big	iri	ee ree
Hair	saç	sach
Brunette	esmer	es mer
Grey	gri	gree
Red	kızıl	kuh zul
Blonde	sarışın	saruh shun
Plait	örgü	ur goo
Auburn	kumral	koom ral
Wave	dalga	dal ga
Bald	kel	kel

Learn Turkish In One Week

English	Turkish	Pronunciation
Face	yüz	yewz
Beautiful	güzel	gew zell
Very beautiful	çok güzel	chok gew zell
Ugly	çirkin	chir keen
Very ugly	çok çirkin	chok chir keen
Attractive	çekici	chek ee jee
Very attractive	çok çekici	chok chek ee jee
Freckle	çil	cheel
Appearance	görünüm	gur roon oom
Glamorous	göz alıcı	gurz a luh juh
Pretty	güzel	gew zell
Wrinkled	kırışık	kuh ruh shuck
Cute	Şirin	shee reen
Handsome	yakışıklı	ya kuh shuck luh
Elegant	zarif	za reef
Brave	cesur	jeh soor
Angry	kızgın	kuz gun
Moustache	bıyık	buh yuk
Beard	sakal	sa kal

Chapters

Learn Turkish In One Week

English	Turkish	Pronunciation
Big nose and long hair	büyük burun ve uzun saç	bew yewk boo roon veh oo zoon sach
Blue eyes	mavi gözlü	mar vee gurz loo
He is very fat	o çok şişman	oe chok sheesh man
A tall man	uzun bir adam	oo zoon beer a dam
Big ears	büyük kulaklar	bew yewk kool ak lar
He is thin	o ince	oe een jeh
Black hair and green eyes	siyah saç ve yeşil gözler	see ya sach veh yeh sheel gurz ler
A big head	bir büyük kafa	bir bew yewk ka fa
A small head	küçük bir kafa	kew chewk beer ka fa
Big hands	büyük eller	bew yewk el ler
She is skinny	o sıska	oe sus ka
Hair is red	saç kırmızı	sach kur muh zuh
He has no hair	saçı yok	sa chuh yok
He is white	o beyaz	oe bay az
White, tall and fat	beyaz uzun ve şişman	bay az oo zoon veh sheesh man
Old and grey	eski ve gri	es kee veh gree
Young and handsome	genç ve yakışıklı	gench veh ya kuh shuk luh
Young	genç	gench
Old	eski	eh skee

Chapters

Learn Turkish In One Week

English	Turkish	Pronunciation
Anxious / worried	endişeli	en dee sheh lee
Arrogant	kibirli	kee bir lee
Clumsy	beceriksiz	beh jeh reek seez
Confused / puzzled	şaşkın	shash kun
Creepy	ürpertici	oor per tee jee
Happy	mutlu	moot loo
Sad	üzgün	ewz gewn
Hungry	aç	ach
Lazy	tembel	tem bell
Grumpy	huysuz	hoy sooz
Nervous	sinirli	seen ir lee
Lonely	yalnız	yal nuz
Jealous	kıskanç	kus kanch
Foolish / silly	aptalca	ap tal ja
An attractive woman	çekici bir kadın	chek ee jee beer ka dun
A tall lady	uzun bir bayan	oo zun beer beye an
She is beautiful	o güzel	oe gew zell
He's cute	o şirin	oe shee reen
She is short	o kısa	oe cuh sa

Chapters

Learn Turkish In One Week

English	Turkish	Pronunciation
Greedy	açgözlü	ach gurz loo
Brave	cesur	jeh soor
Hard working	çalışkan	chal ush kan
Careful	dikkatli	deek kat lee
Nasty	edepsiz	ed ep seez
Sensitive	hassas	hass as
Stubborn	inatçı	een at chuh
Pessimist	kötümser	kur tewm ser
Busy	meşgul	mesh gool
Magnificent	muhteşem	moo teh shem
Cheerful	neşeli	neh sheh lee
Deaf	sağır	saa ur
Blind	kör	kur
Dumb	dilsiz	deel seez
Miserable	sefil	sef eel
Lucy	şanslı	shans luh
Unlucky	şanssız	shans suz
Slow	yavaş	ya vash
Rich	zengin	zen geen

Learn Turkish In One Week

Directions

English	Turkish	Pronunciation
Can I help you	size yardım edebilir miyim	see zeh yar dum ed eh beel ir meem
Where do you want to go	nereye gitmek istersin	neh reh yeh geet mek ee ster seen
Can you help me	bana yardım edebilir misiniz	Ba na yar dum ed eh bill ir mee see niz
Where's the post office	postane nerede	pos tan eh ner eh deh
I'm lost	kayboldum	keye bol doom
Where is the	nerede	ner eh deh
Can I walk there	orada yürüyebilir miyim	or ra da yur uh yeh beel ir meem
Yes you can walk	evet yürüyebilirsiniz	eh vet yur uh yeh beel ir seen eez
No it's too far	hayır çok uzak	heye ur chok oo zak
You can't walk	yürüyemezsin	yur uh yeh mez seen
Is there a bus	otobüs var mı	oh toe bews var muh
Yes there is	evet var	eh vet var
No there isn't	hayır yok	heye ur yok
Direction	yön	yurn
Right	sağ	saa
To the right	sağda	saa da
Left	sol	sol
To the left	solda	sol da
Turn left	sola dön	sol a durn

Chapters

Learn Turkish In One Week

English	Turkish	Pronunciation
Turn right	sağa dön	saa durn
Turn right	sağa dönün	saa dur newn
Turn left	sola dönün	sol a dur newn
On the right hand side	sağ tarafta	saa ta raf ta
On the left hand side	sol tarafta	sol ta raf ta
Here	burada	boo ra da
There	orada	or a da
Go straight	düz git	dewz geet
Go straight	düz gidin	dewz gid een
Ahead	ileride	ee leh ree deh
Back	geride	geh ree deh
Where do you want to go	nereye gitmek istersin	neh reh yeh geet mek eester seen
Far	uzak	oo zak
Close / near	yakın	ya kun
Where is the closest train station	en yakın tren istasyonu nerede	en ya kun tren eestas yon oo neh reh deh
Where's the bus stop	otobüs durağı nerede	oh toe bews duh raa uh neh reh deh
Where's the city centre	şehir merkezi nerede	sheh heer mer kez ee neh reh deh
Street	sokak	soe kak

Chapters

Learn Turkish In One Week

English	Turkish	Pronunciation
Town hall	belediye binası	beh leh dee yeh been a suh
Police station	karakol	ka ra col
Bus terminal	otogar	oh toe gar
Bank	banka	ban ka
Station	istasyon	ee stas yon
Is it far?	uzak mı	oo zak muh
It's near here	buraya yakın	boo ra ya ya kun
It's not far	uzak değil	oo zak deh eel
You're going the wrong way	yanlış yola gidiyorsun	yan lush yoh la geed ee yor soon
Which street?	hangi sokak	han gee soe kak
Walk straight ahead	dümdüz yürüyün	dewm dewz yur uh yewn
Turn back	geri dön	geh ree durn
Turn back	geri dönün	geh ree dur newn
It take five minutes	beş dakika sürer	besh da kee ka sew rer
It takes ten minutes	on dakika sürer	oo da kee ka sew rer
Is there a train?	tren var mı	tren var muh
Yes it's far	evet uzak	eh vet oo zak
No it's near	hayır yakın	heye ur ya kun

Chapters

Learn Turkish In One Week

English	Turkish	Pronunciation
Can you show me on the map	haritada gösterebilir misin	ha ree ta da gur ster eh beel ir mee seen
Map	harita	ha ree ta
On the map	haritada	ha ree ta da
To show	göstermek	gur ster mek
Is there a bank nearby?	yakında banka var mı	ya kun da ban ka var muh
Is there a beach nearby?	yakında plaj var mı	ya kun da plarsh var muh
Is there a hotel nearby?	yakında otel var mı	ya kun da oe tel var muh
Back / backwards	geri	geh ree
Up / upwards	yukarı	yoo ka ruh
Down / downwards	aşağı	a shaa uh
Forward / forwards	ileri	ee lay ree
Excuse me	affedersiniz	a feh der seen eez
Where is strawberry street	çilek caddesi nerede	chee lek ja deh see neh reh deh
I don't know	bilmiyorum	beel mee yor oom
Where are you now?	şimdi tam neredesin	sheem dee tam neh reh deh seen
Immediately	hemen	heh men
Turn left immediately	hemen sola dön	heh men sola durn
North	kuzey	koo zay

Chapters

Learn Turkish In One Week

English	Turkish	Pronunciation
South	güney	gew nay
West	batı	ba tuh
East	doğu	doe oo
Is it this way	bu yönde mı	boo yurn deh muh
Opposite	karşısında	kar shuh sun da
Do you have a map?	haritanız var mı	ha ree tan uz var muh
Thank you very much	çok teşekkür ederim	chok tesh eh kewr eh deh reem
Traffic lights	trafik ışıkları	tra feek ush uck la ruh
Northwest	kuzeybatı	koo zay ba tuh
Northeast	kuzeydoğu	koo zay doe oo
Southwest	güneybatı	gew nay ba tuh
Southeast	güneydoğu	gew nay doe oo
First right	ilk sağ	eelk saa
First left	ilk sol	eelk sol
Second right	ikinci sağ	ee keen jee saa
Second left	ikinci sol	ee keen jee sol
Third right	üçüncü sağ	ewch ewn jew saa
Third left	üçüncü sol	ewch ewn jew sol
Stop	dur	dur

Chapters

City of Ephesus

The well-preserved ruins of Ephesus can be found near the western shores of modern-day Turkey close to Kuşadası. The city was once considered the most important Greek city and the most important trading centre in the Mediterranean region. Throughout history, Ephesus survived multiple attacks and changed hands many times between conquerors. It was also a hotbed of early Christian evangelism and remains an important archaeological site and Christian pilgrimage destination.

In the seventh century B.C., Ephesus fell under the rule of the Lydian Kings and became a thriving city where men and women enjoyed equal opportunities. It was also the birthplace of the renowned philosopher Heraclitus.

Ephesus is one of the largest Roman archaeological sites in the eastern Mediterranean. The spectacular ruins give you a glimpse of how amazing the original city really was.

Ephesus's magnificent splendour became even more fabulous under Roman rule and it was during Augustus's reign that the enormous amphitheater, the library of Celsus, the public space (agora) and the aqueducts were all build.

Ephesus is one of the best Roman ruins anywhere in the Mediterranean and not just in Turkey and a visit to this famous city, which incidentally is the biggest area of excavation in the world, must be top of your list.

Chapters

Learn Turkish In One Week

Doctor

English	Turkish	Pronunciation
Doctor	doktor	dok tor
Medicine	ilaç	eel ach
Tablet	hap	hap
Prescription	reçete	reh cheh teh
Tummy	karın	ka run
Ankle	ayak bileği	eye ack beel ee
Arm	kol	kol
Armpit	koltukaltı	koll too kal tuh
Body	vücut	vew joot
Foot	ayak	eye ak
Hand	el	el
Head	baş	bash
Finger	parmak	par mak
Eye	göz	gurz
Face	yüz	yewz
Leg	bacak	ba jak
Mouth	ağız	aaa uz
Nose	burun	boo roon
Knee	diz	deez

Chapters

Learn Turkish In One Week

English	Turkish	Pronunciation
Ear	kulak	kool ak
Tooth	diş	deesh
Neck	boyun	boy oon
Back	sırt	surt
Eyebrow	kaş	kash
Forehead	alın	a lun
Hair	saç	sach
Shoulder	omuz	oh mooz
Tongue	dil	deel
Heart	kalp	kalp
Brian	beyin	bay een
Bottom	kıç	kuch
Belly	göbek	gur bek
Lip	dudak	doo dak
Toe	ayak parmağı	eye ak par maa uh
Stomach	mide	mee deh
Lung	akciğer	ak jee er
Liver	karaciğer	ka ra jee er
Chest	göğüs	gur ews

Chapters

Learn Turkish In One Week

English	Turkish	Pronunciation
Big toe	ayak başparmağı	eye ak bash par maa uh
Calf	baldır	bal dur
Cheek	yanak	yan ak
Chin	çene	chen eh
Elbow	dirsek	deer sek
Eyelash	kirpik	keer peek
Fist	yumruk	yoom rook
Freckle	çil	cheel
Freckles	çiller	cheel er
Heel	topuk	toh pook
Hip	kalça	kal cha
Index finger	işaret parmağı	ee shar et parm aa uh
Knuckle	parmak eklemi	par mak ek leh mee
Knuckle	boğum	boe oom
Little finger	serçe parmak	ser cheh par mak
Middle finger	orta parmak	or ta par mak
Nail	tırnak	tur nak
Navel	göbek	gur bek
Nostril	burun deliği	boo roon deh lee ee

Chapters

Learn Turkish In One Week

English	Turkish	Pronunciation
Palm	avuçiçi	a vooch ee chee
Shin	incik	een jeek
Skin	cilt	jeelt
Skin	deri	deh ree
Thumb	başparmak	bash par mak
Thigh	uyluk	oy look
Toenail	ayak tırnağı	eye ak turn aa uh
Waist	bel	bel
Wrist	bilek	bee lek
Side	yan	yan
Groin	kasık	ka suck
Muscle	kas	kas
Artery	atardamar	a tar da mar
Throat	boğaz	boe az
Liver	karaciğer	ka ra jee er
Lung	akciğer	ak jee er
Kidney	böbrek	bur breck
Bone	kemik	kem eek
Ear drum	kulak zarı	kool ak za ruh

Chapters

Learn Turkish In One Week

English	Turkish	Pronunciation
Where is there a doctor	nerede bir doktor var	neh reh deh beer dok tor var
Can he come here	buraya gelebilir mi	boo ra ya a gel eh beel ir mee
I'm allergic to	alerjim var	a ler shyeem var
I'm diabetic	şeker hastasıyım	sheh ker hass ta suh yum
I'm pregnant	hamileyim	ham ee leh eem
Can you prescribe something for	için bir reçete yazar misin	eech een eer reh cheh teh yaz ar mee seen
Diarrhoea	ishal	ee sal
Ulcer	ülser	ewl ser
Constipation	kabızlık	kab uz luck
Asthma	astım	as tum
I have a cough	öksürüğüm var	urk sew rew ewm var
I have a headache	baş ağrım var	bash aah rum var
I feel dizzy	başım dönüyor	bash um dur new yor
I feel depressed	bunalıyorum	boon a luh yor oom
I feel tired	yorgun hissediyorum	yor goon hees seh dee yor oom
I feel sick	midem bulanıyor	mee dem bool an uh yor
I can't eat	yemek yiyemiyorum	yeh mek yee yem ee yor oom
I can't sleep	uyuyamıyorum	oy oo yam uh yor oom
I can't move	hareket edemiyorum	ha reh ket eh dem ee yor oom

Chapters

Learn Turkish In One Week

English	Turkish	Pronunciation
I fell	düştüm	dewsh tewm
I have a fever	ateşim var	a tesh eem var
My throat hurts	boğazım ağrıyor	boe az um aa ruh yor
Do you have a fever?	ateşin var mı	a tesh een var muh
Flu	grip	greep
Bed rest	yatak istirahati	ya tack ees tir a ha tee
Take two pills a day	günde iki hap al	gewn deh ee kee hap al
Sprained ankle	burkulan ayak bileği	bur koo lan eye ack beel eh ee
Heart attack	kalp krizi	kalp kree zee
Heat stroke	sıcak çarpması	suh jak charp ma suh
Are you sick?	hasta mısın	has ta muh sun
I don't feel good	iyi hissetmiyorum	ee hees et mee yor oom
What's wrong with you?	neyin var	neh yeen var
I am coughing	ben öksürüğüm	ben urk suh ruh ewm
You have a fever	ateşin var	a tesh een var
I don't want to go to the doctor	doktora gitmek istemiyorum	dock tor a geet mek eestem ee yor um
I feel very tired	çok yorgun hissediyorum	chok yor goon hees ed ee yor oom
Get well soon	gemiş olsun	gech meesh ol soon
What's the matter?	şikayetiniz nedir	shee keye et een iz neh deer

Chapters

Learn Turkish In One Week

English	Turkish	Pronunciation
A little bit	biraz	beer az
Vomiting	kusma	koos ma
Nausea	bulantı	boo lan tuh
No I don't have	hayır yok	heye ur yok
You have a throat infection	boğazınızda enfeksiyon var	boe az un uzda en fek see yon var
Pain killer	ağrı kesici	aa ruh kes ee jee
Here you are	buyrun	boy roon
Rest at home	evde dinlenin	ev deh deen leh neen
I'm sick doctor	hastayım doktor	hass teye um dok tor
I'm cold	üşüyorum	ewsh ew yor oom
My head hurts	başım ağrıyor	ba shum aa ruh yor
My stomach hurts	midem ağrıyor	mee dem aa ruh yor
My arm hurts a lot	kolum çok ağrıyor	koll oom chok aa ruh yor
My leg hurts	bacağım ağrıyor	ba ja um aa ruh yor
My knee hurts	dizim ağrıyor	dee zeem aa ruh yor
My ear hurts	kulağım ağrıyor	kool a um aa ruh yor
I can't sleep	uyuyamıyorum	ooy oo yam uh yor oom
My hand hurts	elim ağrıyor	el eem aa ruh yor
My back hurts	sırtım ağrıyor	sur tum aa ruh yor

Chapters

Learn Turkish In One Week

Drinks

English	Turkish	Pronunciation
Turkish yoghurt drink	ayran	eye ran
Water	su	soo
Cold water	soğuk su	so ook soo
A bottle of water	bir şişe su	beer shee sheh soo
A small bottle of water	küçük bir şişe su	kew chewk beer shee sheh soo
A large bottle of water	büyük bir şişe su	bew yewk beer shee sheh soo
Iced tea	buzlu çay	booz loo cheye
Tea	çay	cheye
Black tea	siyah çay	see ya cheye
With milk	sütle	sewt leh
Tea with milk	çay sütlü	cheye sewt loo
I want tea with milk	sütlü çay istiyorum	sewt loo cheye ee stee yor oom
Apple tea	elma çayı	el ma cheye uh
Tea with lemon	çay limonlu	cheye lee mon loo
Coffee	kahve	kar veh
Black coffee	siyah kahve	see ya kar veh
White coffee	beyaz kahve	bay az kar veh
Instant coffee	neskafe	nes ka feh
Hot milk	sıcak süt	suh jak sewt

Chapters

Learn Turkish In One Week

English	Turkish	Pronunciation
Lemonade	limonata	lee mon a ta
Mineral water	maden suyu	marden soo yoo
Fruit juice	meyve suyu	meh veh soo yoo
Orange juice	portakal suyu	por ta kal soo yoo
Tonic	tonik	ton eek
Peach juice	şeftali suyu	shef ta lee soo yoo
Tomato juice	domates suyu	doe ma tes soo yoo
Coke	kola	coh la
Beer	bira	beer ra
Two beers please	iki bira lütfen	ee kee beer ra lewt fen
Wine	şarap	sha rap
White wine	beyaz şarap	bay az sha rap
Two cold beers please	İki soğuk bira lütfen	ee kee soe ook beer ra lewt fen
Red wine	kırmızı şarap	kur muh zuh sha rap
Rose wine	pembe şarap	pem beh sha rap
Whisky	viski	vee skee
Brandy	brendi	bren dee
Gin	cin	jeen
Cognac	konyak	kon yak

Chapters

Learn Turkish In One Week

English	Turkish	Pronunciation
Rum	rom	rom
Vodka	votka	vot ka
Champagne	şampanya	sham pan ya
Raki	rakı	ra cuh
Sparkling wine	köpüklü şarap	kur pewk loo sha rap
Alcoholic drink	alkollü içki	al kol lew eech kee
Bottle	şişe	shee sheh
Glass	bardak	bar dak
Ice	buz	booz
Lots of ice please	çok buz lütfen	chok booz lewt fen
A glass of white wine please	bir bardak beyaz şarap lütfen	beer bar dak bay az sha rap lewt fen
A bottle of red wine please	bir şişe kırmızı şarap lütfen	beer shee sheh kur muh zuh sha rap lewt fen
A glass of cold beer please	bir bardak soğuk bira lütfen	beer bar dak soe ook beer ra lewt fen
What do you want to drink	ne içmek istiyorsun	neh eech mek ees tee yor soon
Do you want a drink	içecek ister misin	eech eh jek ee ster mee seen
Red or white wine	kırmızı veya beyaz şarap	kur muh zuh veh ya bay az sha rap

Chapters

Learn Turkish In One Week

Emotions

English	Turkish	Pronunciation
Sad	üzgün	ewz gewn
I'm sad	üzgünüm	ooz gew newm
Are you sad?	üzgün müsün	ooz gewn mew soon
Happy	mutlu	moot loo
Guilty	suçlu	sooch loo
Stupid	aptal	ap tal
Exhausted	yorgun	yor goon
Tired	yorgun	yor goon
Headstrong	inatçı	een at chuh
Frightened	korkmuş	cork moosh
Anxious	endişeli	en dee sheh lee
Angry	kızgın	kuz gun
Shy	utangaç	oo tan gach
Jealous	kıskanç	kus kanch
Enthusiastic	hevesli	heh veh slee
Inquisitive	meraklı	mer ak luh
Calm	sakin	sa keen
Relaxed	rahatlamış	ra hat la mush
Calm and relaxed	sakin ve rahatlamış	sar keen veh ra hat la mush

Chapters

Learn Turkish In One Week

English	Turkish	Pronunciation
Energetic	enerjik	en er shyeek
Emotional	duygusal	doo yuh goo sal
Why are you so angry?	neden bu kadar kızgınsın	neh den boo ka dar kuz gun sun
Remorseful	pişman	peesh man
Proud	gururlu	goo rur loo
Proud father	gururlu baba	goo rur loo ba ba
Please calm down	lütfen sakin ol	lewt fen sar keen ol
Grumpy	huysuz	hoy sooz
Grumpy old man	huysuz yaşlı adam	hoy sooz yash luh a dam
Crazy	çılgın	chull gun
He's crazy	o çılgın	oe chull gun
Mad	deli	deh lee
Nervous	sinirli	see nir lee
Surprised	şaşırmış	sha shur mush
Good	iyi	eee
Bad	kötü	kur tew
Alive	canlı	jan luh
Dead	ölü	ur loo
Difficult	zor	zor

Chapters

Learn Turkish In One Week

Dalyan

Dalyan is a popular tourist destination with ancient ruins, mud baths and loggerhead sea turtles breeding grounds. It is a Turkish town in the Muğla province, located between the districts of Marmaris and Fethiye on the south west coast.

Dalyan is surrounded by mountains which protects it from strong winds making it extremely hot, especially in the summer months. Years ago it was an old fishing village but tourism has now become the main source of income for the local people.

Iztuzu beach is breathtaking with shallow waters and a long sandy beach making it perfect for families.

Shopping at Dalyan market is lots of fun and the town really comes to life. A walk through the fruit and veg stalls is a must to soak up the wonderful atmosphere.

Boats trips are plentiful where you'll pass the magnificent Dalyan rock tombs on the way to the famous Dalyan mud baths. Or jump a water taxi and head in the opposite direction for a chilled day on Iztuzu Beach.

Dalyan has something for everyone and a stay at this beautiful Turkish town will not disappoint.

Chapters

Learn Turkish In One Week

Family

English	Turkish	Pronunciation
Family	aile	eye leh
Relation / relative	akraba	ak ra ba
Uncle	amca	am ja
Uncle	dayı	deye uh
Aunty	teyze	tay zeh
Aunt	hala	ha la
Father	baba	ba ba
Mother	anne	an neh
Brother	erkek kardeş	er kek car desh
Sister	kız kardeş	kuz car desh
Son	oğul	oe ool
Daughter	kız evlat	kuz ev lat
Grandfather	büyük baba	bew yewk ba ba
Grandfather	dede	deh deh
Grandmother	büyükanne	bew yewk an neh
Grandmother	anneanne	an neh an neh
Grandson	erkek torun	er kek toe roon
Granddaughter	kız torun	kuz toe roon
Grandchild	torun	toe roon

Chapters

Learn Turkish In One Week

English	Turkish	Pronunciation
Sister-in-law	baldız	bal duz
Brother-in-law	kayınbirader	keye un beer a der
Mother-in-law	kaynana	keye nan a
Father-in-law	kayınpeder	keye un pay der
Husband	koca	coe ja
Wife	karı	ka ruh
Wife	eş	esh
Child	çocuk	choe jook
Children	çocuklar	choe jook lar
Cousin	kuzen	koo zen
Step mother	üvey anne	oo vay an neh
Step father	üvey baba	oo vay ba ba
Niece	kızı yeğen	kuz yeh en
Nephew	erkek yeğen	er kek yeh en
Bride	gelin	geh leen
Bridegroom	damat	da mat
Twin	ikiz	ee keez
Adult	yetişkin	yeh tee sh keen
Parents	ebeveynler	eb eh vayn ler

Chapters

Learn Turkish In One Week

Farm

English	Turkish	Pronunciation
Horse	at	at
Cow	inek	een ek
Farmer	çiftçi	cheeft chee
Farm	çiftlik	cheeft leek
Animals	hayvanlar	heye van lar
Bucket	kova	koe va
Bull	boğa	boe a
Field	alan	a lan
Duck	ördek	ur dek
Duckling	ördek yavrusu	ur dek yav roo soo
Barn	ahır	a hur
Hay	saman	sa man
Chicken	tavuk	ta vook
Chicken	piliç	peel eech
Egg	yumurta	yoo moo ta
Sheep	koyun	koy oon
Goat	keçi	keh chee
Turkey	hindi	heen dee
Rabbit	tavşan	tav shan

Chapters

Learn Turkish In One Week

English	Turkish	Pronunciation
Mouse	fare	far eh
Rat	sıçan	suh chan
Owl	baykuş	beye koosh
Cat	kedi	keh dee
Dog	köpek	kur pek
Donkey	eşek	esh ek
Farmhouse	çiftlik evi	cheeft leek ev ee
Fence	çit	cheet
Goose	kaz	kaz
Milk	süt	sewt
Scarecrow	korkuluk	kor koo look
Tractor	traktör	trac tur
Vegetables	sebzeler	seb zeh ler
Land	arazi	a rar zee
Lamb	kuzu	koo zoo
Bee	bal arısı	bal aa ruh suh
Honey	bal	bal
Bee hive	arı kovanı	a ruh koe van uh
Frog	kurbağa	kur ba aa

Chapters

Learn Turkish In One Week

Food

English	Turkish	Pronunciation
Soup	çorba	chor ba
Pea soup	bezelye Çorbası	bez el yeh chor ba suh
Tomato soup	domates çorbası	doe ma tes chor ba suh
Mushroom soup	mantar çorbası	man tar chor ba suh
Lentil soup	mercimek çorbası	mer jee mek chor ba suh
Vegetable soup	sebze çorbası	seb zeh chor ba suh
Chicken soup	tavuk çorbası	tav ook chor ba suh
Salad dressing	salata sosu	sal a ta soh soo
Green salad	yeşil salata	yeh sheel sal a ta
Shrimp salad	karides salatası	ka ree des sal a ta suh
Tomato salad	domates salatası	doe ma tes sal a ta suh
Cheese	peynir	pay neer
White cheese	beyaz peynir	bay az pay neer
Cream cheese	krem peynir	krem pay neer
Olives	zeytin	zay teen
Salami	salam	sa lam
Salads	salatalar	sal a ta lar
Appetizers	mezeler	meh zeh ler
Fried potatoes	patates kızartma	pa ta tes kuz art ma

Chapters

Learn Turkish In One Week

English	Turkish	Pronunciation
French fries	patates tava	pa ta tes ta va
Roasted potatoes	patates fırında	pa ta tes fur un da
Mashed potatoes	patates püre	pa ta tes pew reh
Caviar	havyar	hav yar
Mussels	midye	meed yeh
Pickles	turşu	toor shoo
Pickled cucumber	salatalık turşusu	sal at a luk toor shoo soo
Pickled peppers	biber turşusu	bee ber toor shoo soo
Cold chicken	soğuk tavuk	soe ook tav ook
Main course	ana yemekler	an a yeh mek ler
Lamb chops	kuzu pirzola	koo zoo peer zoe la
Veal cutlets	dana pirzola	dan a peer zoe la
Mixed grill	karışık ızgara	ka ra shuk uz ga ra
Steak	biftek	beef tek
Rare	az pişmiş	az peesh meesh
Medium	orta pişmiş	or ta peesh meesh
Well done	çok pişmiş	chok peesh meesh
Grilled meatballs	ızgara köfte	uz ga ra kurf teh
Roast chicken	tavuk kızartma	tav uk kuz art ma

Chapters

Learn Turkish In One Week

English	Turkish	Pronunciation
Roast chicken	piliç kızartma	peel eech kuz art ma
Döner kebap	döner kebap	dur ner keh bap
Shish kebap	şiş kebap	sheesh keh bap
Omelette	omlet	om let
Cheese omelette	peynirli omlet	pay neer lee om let
Spaghetti	spagetti	spa geh tee
Macaroni	makarna	ma kar na
Chinese spring rolls	çin böreği	cheen bur eh ree
Sea food	deniz mahsulleri	deh neez ma sool leh ree
Octopus	ahtapot	aa ta pot
Trout	alabalık	a la ba luk
Fish	balık	ba luk
Oyster	istiridye	ees tee reed yeh
Squid	kalamar	kal a mar
Shrimp	karides	ka ree des
Swordfish	kılıçbalığı	kul uch ba luh uh
Lobster	ıstakoz	us ta koz
Bass	levrek	lev rek
Haddock	mezgit	mez geet

Chapters

Learn Turkish In One Week

English	Turkish	Pronunciation
Mussel	midye	meed yeh
Sardine	sardalya	sar dal ya
Salmon	somon	soh mon
Mackerel	uskumru	oos koom roo
Crab	yengeç	yen gech
Desert	tatlı	tat luh
Rice pudding	sütlaç	sewt lach
Pie	turta	toor ta
Cake	pasta	pa sta
Jelly	jöle	shjur leh
Chocolate	çikolata	chee koe la ta
Ice cream	dondurma	don dur ma
Vanilla	vanilya	van eel ya
Strawberry ice cream	çilekli dondurma	chee lek lee don dur ma
Strawberry	çilek	chee lek
Cream caramel	krem karamel	crem ka ra mel
Pepper	biber	bee ber
Salt	tuz	tooz
Vinegar	sirke	seer keh

Chapters

Learn Turkish In One Week

English	Turkish	Pronunciation
Mustard	hardal	har dal
Black pepper	karabiber	ka ra bee ber
Cummin	kimyon	keem yon
Parsley	maydanoz	meye da noz
Mint	nane	nar neh
Garlic	sarımsak	sa rum sak
Cinnamon	tarçın	tar chun
Salt and pepper	tuz ve biber	tooz veh bee ber
Ginger	zencefil	zen jeh feel
Raw	çiğ	chee
Fried	kızartma	kuh zart ma
Beef	sığır eti	sur eh tee
Chicken	tavuk	ta vook
Chicken	piliç	peel eech
Lamb	kuzu	koo zoo
Sausage	sosis	soh sees
Steak	biftek	beef tek
Turkey	hindi	heen dee
Bread	ekmek	ek mek

Chapters

Learn Turkish In One Week

English	Turkish	Pronunciation
Pasta	makarna	ma car na
Rice	pirinç	pee reench
Rice	pilav	pee lav
Mayonnaise	mayonez	meye on ez
Egg	yumurta	yoo moo ta
Yogurt	yoğurt	yoe urt
Milk	süt	sewt
Sugar	şeker	sheh ker
Ketchup	ketçap	ket chap
Sandwich	sandviç	sand veech
Breakfast	kahvaltı	karv al tuh
Lunch	öğle yemeği	ur leh yem eh ee
Dinner	akşam yemeği	ak sham yeh meh ee
Meal	yemek	yeh meck
Food	yiyecek	yee yeh jek
Butter	tereyağı	teh reh aa uh
Meat	et	et
Bean	fasulye	fa sool yeh
Crackers	krakerler	krack er ler

Chapters

Learn Turkish In One Week

English	Turkish	Pronunciation
Sauce	sos	sos
Table cloth	masa örtüsü	ma sa ur tew soo
Napkin	peçete	peh cheh teh
Glass	bardak	bar dak
Saltshaker	tuzluk	tooz look
Peppershaker	biberlik	bee ber leek
Sugar bowl	şekerlik	sheh ker leek
Coffee pot	cezve	jez veh
Tray	tepsi	tep see
Ham	jambon	shyam bon
Meatball	köfte	kurf teh
Pork	domuz eti	doh mooz eh tee
Pancake	gözleme	gurz leh meh
A little sugar	biraz şeker	beer az sheh ker
Lots of sugar please	çok şeker lütfen	chok sheh ker lewt fen
Corn	mısır	muh sur
Turkish delight	lokum	loe koom
Sliced bread	dilimlenmiş ekmek	dee leem len meesh ek mek
Delicious	lezzetli	lay zet lee

Chapters

Learn Turkish In One Week

Fethiye

Fethiye is one of my favourite places and is a city and district of Muğla with a population of more than 162 000 back in 2019. It is located on the edge of the sea on the site of the ancient city or Telmessos. The historic Hellenistic theatre is often overlook due to the shops, cafes and seaside restaurants bursting with life.

Fethiye has breathtaking landscapes, a low cost of living, excellent property prices and friendly local people making it a perfect place to live or holiday.

Close by are the resorts of Çalis, Hisarönü and Ölüdeniz which make Fethiye a perfect location for exploring further a field.

Fethiye has fabulous hotels and a large marina where there is daily hydrofoil service to Rhodes and other parts of Turkey.

Take a boat trip from the harbour and visit the 12 surrounding islands or climb to the Lycian Rock Tombs nestled in the enormous mountains protecting this busy city.

There is a market every week and a shop for for every need you may have from tools, food, shoe repairs, curtains, wedding, electrical. You name it and they will have it. Go in and negotiate a price and the product you require will be delivered that very day. The service is exceptional.

Everyone should visit Fethiye when in Turkey. I guarantee you won't be disappointed.

Chapters

Learn Turkish In One Week

Fruits

English	Turkish	Pronunciation
Pineapple	ananas	an a nas
Pear	armut	ar moot
Blackberry	böğürtlen	buh urt len
Strawberry	çilek	chee lek
Apple	elma	el ma
Plum	erik	eh reek
Grapefruit	greyfurt	gray furt
Coconut	hindistan cevizi	hin dee stan jev ee zee
Water melon	karpuz	kar pooz
Melon	kavun	kav oon
Apricot	kayısı	keye uh suh
Cherry	kiraz	kee raz
Tangerine	mandalina	man da leen a
Banana	muz	mooz
Orange	portakal	por ta kal
Peach	şeftali	shef ta lee
Grape	üzüm	oo zoom
Pomegranate	nar	nar
Fig	incir	een jeer

Chapters

Learn Turkish In One Week

General Phrases

English	Turkish	Pronunciation
Hello	merhaba	mer ha ba
Hi	selam	seh lam
Good morning	günaydın	gewn eye dun
Good day	iyi günler	ee goon ler
Have a nice day	iyi günler	ee goon ler
Good afternoon	tünaydın	toon eye dun
Good evening	iyi akşamlar	ee ack sham lar
Good night	iyi geceler	ee geh gel er
Goodbye	güle güle	gew lay gew lay
Goodbye	hoşça kal	hosh cha cal
See you	görüşürüz	gur ruh shur ruz
See you later	sonra görüşürüz	son ra gur ruh shur ruz
Yes	evet	eh vet
No	hayır	h eye ur
Please	lütfen	lewt fen
Thanks	teşekkürler	teh shek kur ler
Thank you	teşekkür ederim	teh shek kur eh deh reem
Thank you very much	çok teşekkür ederim	chok teh shek kur eh deh reem
Not at all	bir şey değil	beer shay deh eel

Chapters

Learn Turkish In One Week

English	Turkish	Pronunciation
Excuse me	affedersiniz	a feh der seen eez
Help	imdat	eem dat
Good luck	iyi şanslar	ee shans lar
Not bad	fena değil	fena deh eel
Very good	çok iyi	chok ee
Good	iyi	ee
Wonderful	harika	ha ree ka
Be quiet	sessiz olun	ses seez ol oon
Listen	dinle	deen leh
Listen to me	beni dinle	beh nee deen leh
How are you?	nasılsın	na sull sun
I'm fine thanks	iyiyim, teşekkürler	eem teh shek kur ler
I'm good	iyiyim	eem
How's life?	ne var ne yok	neh var neh yoe k
So so	şöyle böyle	shur leh bur leh
How's it going?	nasıl gidiyor	na sull gee dee yor
No thank you	hayır teşekkürler	heye ur teh shek kur ler
Very well thank you	çok iyi teşekkür ederim	chok ee teh shek kur eh deh reem
That one please	şu lütfen	shoo lewt fen

Chapters

Learn Turkish In One Week

English	Turkish	Pronunciation
See you tomorrow	yarın görüşürüz	ya run gur ruh shur uz
See you on Monday	pazartesi görüşürüz	pa zar teh see gur ruh shur uz
See you in June	haziran görüşürüz	ha zee ran gur ruh shur uz
Maybe tomorrow	belki yarın	bel kee ya run
In ten minutes	on dakika içinde	on da kee ka eech een deh
In two minutes	iki dakika içinde	ee kee da kee ka eech een deh
Five more minutes	beş dakika daha	besh da kee ka da ha
In one hour	bir saat içinde	beer sart eech een deh
In two days	iki gün içinde	ee kee gewn eech in deh
Next week	gelecek hafta	gel eh jek haf ta
This week	bu hafta	boo haf ta
This weekend	bu haftasonu	boo haf ta son oo
Next year	gelecek yıl	gel eh jek yul
Yes please	evet lütfen	eh vet lewt fen
Welcome everyone	herkese hoş geldiniz	her keh seh hosh gel deen iz
Close the window	pencereyi kapat	pen jeh reh yee ka pat
Close the door	kapıyı kapat	ka puh yuh ka pat
Sit down	otur	oe toor
Stand up	kalk	kalk

Chapters

Learn Turkish In One Week

English	Turkish	Pronunciation
I don't know	bilmiyorum	beel mee yor oom
You're welcome	rica ederim	ree jar eh deh reem
How old are you?	kaç yaşındasın	kach ya shun da sun
I am twenty	yirmi yaşındayım	yir mee ya shun deye um
Age	yaş	yash
Your age	yaşın	ya shun
What are you doing today?	bugün ne yapıyorsun	boo gewn neh yap uh yor soon
Perhaps	belki	bel kee
Of course	tabii	ta bee
Welcome	hoşgeldiniz	hosh gel deen iz
OK	tamam	ta mam
Really	sahi mi	sar hee mee
Sorry	üzgünüm	ooz gewn oom
I'm sorry	özür dilerim	ooz ur dee leh reem
What a pity	ne yazık	neh ya zuk
Where are the toilets?	tuvaletler nerede	too va let ler neh reh deh
Speak more slowly	daha yavaş konuş	da ha ya vash kon oosh
More slowly	daha yavaş	da ha ya vash
Do you understand?	anlıyor musun	an luh yor moo soon

Chapters

Learn Turkish In One Week

English	Turkish	Pronunciation
Do you understand Turkish	Türkçe anlıyor musun	turk cheh an luh yor moo soon
Excuse me where is?	affedersiniz nerede	a feh der seen iz neh reh deh
Do you speak English?	ingilizce konuşuyor musun	een gee leez jeh kon oo shor moo sun
Delicious	lezzetli	lez zet lee
Delicious	nefis	neh feece
Shut up	kapa çeneni	ka pa cheh neh nee
Shush	sus	soo s
I'm Turkish	ben Türküm	ben tur kewm
We're Turkish	biz türküz	beez tur kewz
I'm English	ben ingilizim	ben een gee leez eem
We're English	biz ingiliziz	beez een gee leez iz
I am lost	kayboldum	keye boll doom
Not bad	eh işte	eh eesh teh
Come in	içeri gir	ee cheh ree geer
Come in please	içeri gir lütfen	ee cheh ree geer lewt fen
What do you want?	ne istiyorsun	neh ees tee yor soon
Come	gel	gel
Go	git	geet
Drink	iç	eech

Chapters

Learn Turkish In One Week

English	Turkish	Pronunciation
My name is Geoff	benim adım geoff	ben eem a dum Jef
What's your name?	adınız ne	a dun uz neh
What's your name?	adın nedir	a dun neh deer
What's your surname?	soyadınız ne	soy a dun uz neh
My surname is Jackson	benim soyadım jackson	ben eem soy a dum jack son
This is my friend	bu benim arkadaşım	boo ben eem ar ka da shum
Eat	ye	yeh
Call me	beni ara	ben ee a ra
I'm a little late	biraz geç kaldım	beer az gech kal dum
What's the matter?	sorun ne	soh roon neh
Why are you late?	neden geç kaldın	neh den gech kal dun
Where are you from?	nerelisin	neh reh lee seen
I'm from England	ben İngiltere'den geliyorum	ben een geel teh reh den gel ee yor oom
I'm not from Turkey	ben türkiyeden değilim	ben tur kee yeh den deh eel im
I'm not Turkish	ben türk değilim	ben turk deh eel im
Beautiful	güzel	gew zel
Never	asla	ass la
Excuse me where is the beach	affedersiniz plaj nerede	a feh der seen iz pee larsh neh reh deh

Chapters

Learn Turkish In One Week

English	Turkish	Pronunciation
You don't say	yapma ya	yap ma ya
Come on	hadi	ha dee
Jackass	lan	lan
What are you talking about jackass	ne diyorsun lan	neh dee yor soon lan
What's your name	adın ne	a dun neh
Wait a moment	dur bir dakika	dur beer da kee ka
Congratulations	tebrikler	teh breek ler
To be or not to be	olmak ya da olmamak	ol mak ya da ol ma mak
Stop talking	kes konuşmayı	kes kon oosh may uh
Cut it out	kes şunu	kes shun oo
I don't want to talk to you	seninle konuşmak istemiyorum	sen een leh kon oosh mak ee stem ee yor oom
I'm upset	sinirliyim	see neer lee yim
Get well soon	geçmiş olsun	gech meesh ol sun
Don't mind	boş ver	bosh ver
I'm hungry as a wolf	kurt gibi açım	kurt gee bee a chum
I am always very hungry	ben her zaman çok açım	ben her za man chok a chum
I've waited for too long	beklemekten ağaç oldum	bek leh mek ten aach ol doom
God bless you (when sneezing)	çok yaşa	chok ya sha

Chapters

Learn Turkish In One Week

English	Turkish	Pronunciation
I beg you	n'olur	no lor
I've got a headache because of the noise	başım şişti	ba shum sheesh tee
Bla bla / etc etc	falan filan	fa lan fee lan
No way / really	yok artık	yoek ar tuk
How lovely	ne güzel	neh gew zell
Where do you work	nerede çalışıyorsun	ner eh deh chal ush uh yor soon
Where do you live	nerede yaşıyorsun	ner eh deh yash uh yor soon
What's your telephone number	telefon numaran ne	tel eh fon noo ma ran neh
I'm so sorry	çok üzgünüm	chok ooz gewn um
I have an objection	bir itirazım var	beer ee tee raz um var
I'd love to	çok isterim	chok ee steh reem
Where are you going?	nereye gidiyorsun	neh reh yeh gee dee yor soon
Happy birthday	doğum günün kutlu olsun	doh oom gew newm koot loo ol soon
Happy New Year	yeni yılınız kutlu olsun	yeh nee yul un uz koot loo ol soon
Happy Easter	iyi Paskalyalar	ee pas kal ya lar
Merry Christmas	mutlu Noeller	moot loo no el ler
I understand	anlıyorum	an luh yor oom
Can I sit here	buraya oturabilir miyim	boo ra ya oh too ra bil ir meem

Chapters

Learn Turkish In One Week

English	Turkish	Pronunciation
I'm busy	meşgulüm	mesh goo lewm
Nothing	hiç bir şey	heech beer shay
I don't want anything	hiç bir şey istemiyorum	heech bir shay ee stem ee yor oom
Never mind	boş ver	bosh ver
Don't worry	endişelenmeyin	en dee shel en may een
I do apologize	özür dilerim	ur zur dee leh reem
All right	tamam	ta mam
It doesn't matter	fark etmez	fark et mez
I'll miss you	seni özleyeceğim	sen ee urz lay eh jeh eem
What's this?	bu nedir	boo neh deer
What is that?	şu nedir	shoo neh deer
What is it?	o nedir	oe neh deer
I don't understand	anlamıyorum	an lam uh yor oom
Could you write it down	yazabilir misiniz	yaz a beel ir mee seen iz
I know a little English	biraz ingilizce biliyorum	bir az een gee leez jeh beel ee yor um
I speak a little English	biraz İngilizce konuşuyorum	bir az een gee leez jeh kon uh shor um
I know a little Turkish	biraz türkçe biliyorum	bir az turk cheh beel ee yor oom
Do you understand me	beni anlıyor musun	ben ee an luh yor muh soon
I understand you	sizi anlıyorum	see zee an luh yor oom

Chapters

Learn Turkish In One Week

English	Turkish	Pronunciation
Certainly	elbette	el beh teh
Can I have	alabilir miyim	a la beel ir meem
Can I open	açabilir miyim	ach a beel ir meem
Can you tell	söyleyebilir misin	soy leh yeh beel ir mee seen
Can you show	gösterebilir misin	gur ster eh beel ir mee seen
I want	istiyorum	ee stee yor oom
Can you help me please	bana yardım edebilir misiniz lütfen	ban a yar dum ed eh bil ir mee seen iz lewt fen
I want wine	şarap istiyorum	sha rap ee stee yor oom
I want to go	gitmek istiyorum	geet mek ee stee yor oom
I want to go to Fethiye	Fethiyeye gitmek istiyorum	fet ee yeh yeh geet mek ee stee yor oom
I want to go home	eve gitmek istiyorum	ev eh geet mek ee stee yor oom
What's this in English	bunun ingilizcesi nedir	boo noon een gee leez jeh see neh deer
Where is your wife?	karın nerede	ka run ner eh deh
She's in the pool	o havuzda	oe hav ooz da
She's in the kitchen	o mutfakta	oe moo fak ta
She's at home	o evde	oe ev deh
What time is it?	saat kaç	sart kach
Where is?	nerede	ner eh deh

Chapters

Learn Turkish In One Week

English	Turkish	Pronunciation
Where is the nearest	en yakın nerede	en ya kun ner eh deh
Where is the nearest beach?	en yakın plaj nerede	en ya kun pee larsh ner eh deh
Where can I get	nereden abilirim	ner eh den a bee leer eem
Where can I get bread?	nereden ekmek alabilirim	ner eh den ek mek a la bee leer eem
It's one O'clock	saat bir	sart beer
It's two O'clock	saat iki	sart ee kee
In the morning	sabahleyin	sa ba lay een
In the evening	akşamleyin	ak sham lay een
You're late	geç kaldınız	gech kal dun uz
I'm sorry I'm late	özür dilerim geciktim	urz ur dee leh reem geh jeek teem
I'm sorry my love	özür dilerim aşkım	urz ur dee leh reem ash kum
I know	biliyorum	bee lee yor oom
I think so	sanırım	san uh rum
I don't think so	sanmıyorum	san muh yor oom
I'm sure	eminim	em een eem
I'm not sure	emin değilim	em een deh eel im
I hope so	umarım	oom a rum
You're right	haklısınız	hak luh sun uz

Chapters

Learn Turkish In One Week

English	Turkish	Pronunciation
You're mistaken	yanışlının var	yan ush lun un var
I see	anlıyorum	an luh yor oom
We'll see	göreceğiz	gur reh jeh eez
That's good news	iyi haber	ee ha ber
Wait and see	bekle ve gör	bek leh veh gur
My mistake	benim hatam	ben eem ha tam
Have a nice trip	iyi yolculuklar	ee yol joo look lar
Have a nice time	iyi eğlenceler	ee eh len jel er
It's possible	olabilir	oh la beel ir
Impossible	olamaz	oe la maz
I'm afraid	korkarım	kor ka rum
I object	itiraz ediyorum	ee tee raz eh dee yor oom
Where were you born?	nerede doğdunuz	ner eh deh doe oe doon uz
What's your religion	dininiz nedir	deen een iz neh deer
I'm Muslim	ben Müslümanım	ben mews lewm a num
I'm Catholic	ben katoliğim	ben kat oe lee eem
When were you born	ne zaman doğdunuz	neh za man doe doon ooz
What's your job?	işiniz nedir	ee shee niz neh deer
What do you do?	ne iş yapıyorsunuz	neh eesh yap uh yor soon uz

Chapters

Learn Turkish In One Week

English	Turkish	Pronunciation
Do you have any children?	çocuklarınız var mı	choe jook la run uz var muh
I've got one son	bir oğlum var	beer oel oom var
And	ve	veh
I've got two daughters	iki kızım var	ee kee kuh zum var
Or	veya	vay a
Let's go	hadi gidelim	ha dee geed eh leem
Let's go home	hadi eve gidelim	ha dee ev eh geed eh leem
Let's go together	hadi birlikte gidelim	ha dee beer leek teh geed eh leem
And you	ya sen	ya sen
I love you	seni seviyorum	sen ee sev ee yor oom
I love you so much	seni çok seviyorum	sen ee chok sev ee yor oom
I love you too	ben de seni seviyorum	ben deh sen ee sev ee yor oom
I love you more	seni daha fazla seviyorum	sen ee da ha faz la sev ee yor oom
My love	aşkım	ash kum
Good morning my love	günaydın aşkım	gewn eye dun ash kum
Good night and sweet dreams	iyi geceler ve tatlı rüyalar	ee geh jel er vey tat luh roo ya lar
No smoking	sigara içmek yasaktır	see gara eech mek yas ak tur
Do you love me?	beni seviyor musun	ben ee sev ee yor moo soon

Chapters

Learn Turkish In One Week

English	Turkish	Pronunciation
I know you	seni biliyorum	sen ee beel ee yor oom
I know	biliyorum	beel ee yor oom
What are you doing?	ne yapıyorsun	neh yap uh yor soon
I want you	seni istiyorum	sen ee ee stee yor oom
I want to see you	seni görmek istiyorum	sen ee gur mek ee stee yor oom
I understand	anlıyorum	an luh yor oom
Do you understand English?	ingilizce anlıyor musun	een gee leez jeh an luh yor moo soon
Do you understand now?	şimdi anlıyor musun	sheem dee an luh yor moo soon
Do you like football?	futboldan hoşlanır mısın	foot bol dan hosh lan ur muh sun
Do you like music?	müzikdan hoşlanır mısın	mew zeek dan hosh lan ur muh sun
I don't like it	sevmem	sev mem
I like it very much	çok severim	chok seh veh reem
How nice to see you	seni görmek ne hoş	sen ee gur mek neh hosh
I'm glad you could come	geldiğinize sevindim	gel dee een iz eh sev een dim
Let me take your coat	paltonuzu alayım	pal ton oo zoo al a yum
Please sit down	lütfen oturun	lewt fen oe too roon
Would you like some tea / coffee	çay kahve ister misin	cheye ka feh ee ster mee seen

Chapters

Learn Turkish In One Week

English	Turkish	Pronunciation
Do you smoke	sigara içiyor musunuz	see ga ra eech ee yor moo soon uz
Are you free tomorrow?	yarın boş musunuz	ya run bosh moo soon ooz
Are you free tomorrow morning?	yarın sabah boş musunuz	ya run sa ba bosh moo son ooz
Yes I'm free	evet boşum	eh vet bosh oom
That's very kind of you	çok naziksiniz	chok na zeek seen eez
Have a nice day my love	iyi günler aşkım	ee gewn ler ash kum
Please my love	lütfen aşkım	lewt fen ash kum
How much do you have?	ne kadar var	neh ka dar var
I've lost my key	anahtarımı kaybettim	an a ta rum uh keye bet teem
Is there a problem?	bir sorun mu var	beer soe roon moo var
There's no water	su yok	soo yok
The shower doesn't work	duş çalışmıyor	doosh chal ush muh yor
What's your room number?	oda numaranız kaç	or da noo ma ran ooz kach
Is the bill ready?	hesap hazır mı	her sap haz ur muh
I want more	daha fazla istiyorum	da ha faz la ee stee yor oom
I don't want anything	hiç bir şey istemiyorum	heech beer shay ee stem ee yor oom
Goodbye my love	hoşçakal aşkım	hosh cha kal ash kum

Chapters

Göcek

Göcek is situated about 27km from Fethiye and tucked into a picturesque coves surrounded by magnificent mountains covered in pine trees. It is popular with sailors and yachts and is proud of it's international yachting centre and five first-class marinas.

The region has the status of national park and is under the governments protection. It used to be a quiet sleepy fishing village but is now a popular, upmarket destination for tourists and sailors. There's an abundance of interesting shops and fabulous restaurants to make a visit a must during your stay in Turkey.

Göcek town is surrounded by 12 islands and is famous for its natural beauty among sailors.

It is also a popular destination for many well known film stars and celebrities who love coming to this beautiful little town to avoid the crowds that are associated with the more popular resorts.

Property prices in Göcek increase every year due to its exclusive element and natural beauty.

There are plenty of boat trips to choose from and the ancient ruins of Kalimce can be seen under the water in nearby bays.

A visit to Turkey is not complete unless you have made a stop in Göcek

Chapters

Learn Turkish In One Week

Hobbies

English	Turkish	Pronunciation
Football	futbol	foot bol
Boxing	boks	box
Gymnastics	jimnastik	shyeem na steek
Horse racing	at yarışı	at ya ruh shuh
Sports	spor	spor
Mountaineering	dağcılık	daa juh luk
To draw	çizmek	cheez mek
I like drawing pictures	resim çizmeyi severim	reh seem cheez meh yee seh ver reem
Surfing the net	nette sörf yapmak	neh teh surf yap mak
Play a musical instrument	bir müzik aleti çalmak	bir mew zeek a leh tee chal mak
Play chess	satranç oynamak	sat ranch oy na mak
Swim	yüzmek	yewz mek
I read books	kitap okuyorum	kee tap oe koo yor oom
Painting	resim yapmak	reh seem yap mak
Fishing	balık tutmak	ba luk toot mak
Cooking	yemek pişirme	yeh mek peesh ir meh
Swimming	yüzme	yewz meh
Free time	boş zaman	bosh za man
Reading	okumak	oe koo mak

Chapters

Learn Turkish In One Week

English	Turkish	Pronunciation
Watching TV	televizyon izlemek	teh leh veez yon eez leh mek
Playing cards	kart oynamak	cart oy na mak
Playing computer games	bilgisayar oyunu oynamak	beel gee seye ar oy oo noo oy na mak
Playing board games	masa oyunu oynamak	ma sa oy oo noo oy na mak
Playing the guitar	gitar çalma	gee tar chal mak
Listening to music	müzik dinlemek	mewz eek deen leh mek
Painting	boyama yapmak	boy a ma yap mak
Singing	şarkı söyleme	shar kuh soy leh meh
Dancing	dans etmek	dans et mek
Diving	dalış yapmak	da lush yap mak
Hiking	doğa yürüyüşü	doe a yur oo yoo shew
Walking	yürüyüş yapmak	yur uh yoosh yap mak
Running	koşmak	kosh mak
Ice skating	buz pateni yapmak	booz pa ten ee yap mak
Skiing	kayak yapmak	keye ak yap mak
Climbing	tırmanış yapmak	tur man ush yap mak
Riding a bike	bisiklet sürmek	bee see clet sur mek
Taking pictures	fotoğraf çekmek	foe toe graf chek mek
Going to the restaurant	restorana gitmek	ray stor an a geet mek

Chapters

Learn Turkish In One Week

Hisarönü

Hisarönü is a popular resort, high in the mountains that really comes alive at night. Clubs and bars are plentiful along the main street and you'll often come across many of the locals dancing on the bar to entice people in. There's foam parties, karaoke, cabaret, drag acts and lots more to cater for everyones taste.

There's no beach in Hisarönü, but Ölüdeniz is a short bus ride down the mountain. If you're feeling energetic then a breathtaking walk is for you. The views on the way down are amazing so take your camera. Walking down is fun but I highly recommend taking the bus on the way back.

There's a market every Monday with a bargain to be had, but be prepared to haggle. The items are mostly fake, but good fakes. Do not pay the first price they tell you because they expect to be knocked down. You know you've got a good price when they stop smiling and growl a little. All part of the game!

Chapters

Learn Turkish In One Week

Holidays

English	Turkish	Pronunciation
Plane	uçak	oo chak
Suitcase	bavul	ba vool
Passport	pasaport	pass a port
Taxi	taksi	tak see
Hotel	otel	oe tel
Beach	plaj	pee larsh
Sea	deniz	den eez
Restaurant	restoran	res toh ran
Restaurant	lokanta	loe kan ta
Tourist	turist	too reest
Ice cream	dondurma	don dur ma
Sun cream	güneş kremi	gewn esh crem ee
Sun	güneş	gewn esh
Sunburn	güneş yanığı	gewn esh yan uh
Swimming pool	yüzme havuzu	yewz meh hav oo zoo
Cable car	teleferik	teh leh feh reek
Bucket and spade	kova ve kürek	koe va veh kew rek
Money	para	pa ra
Love	aşk	ashk

Chapters

Learn Turkish In One Week

Hospital

English	Turkish	Pronunciation
Hospital	hastane	hass tan eh
You look bad	kötü görünüyorsun	kur too guh rewn oo yor soon
I have stomach ache	karnım çok ağrıyor	kar num chok aa ruh yor
Nurse	hemşire	hem shee reh
Doctor	doktor	dok tor
Entrance	giriş	gee reesh
Exit	çıkış	chuck ush
Where is the nearest hospital	en yakın hastane nerede	en ya kun hass tan eh ner eh deh
I have an appointment with doctor	doktorla randevum var	dok tor la ran deh voom var
I have an appointment at 10 O'clock	saat onda randevum var	saat on da ran deh voom var
Please wait in waiting room	lütfen bekleme odasında bekleyin	lewt fen bek leh meh oh da sun da bek lay een
The doctor is coming straight away	doktor hemen geliyor	dok tor heh men gel ee yor
Do you have pain	ağrınız var mı	aa run uz var muh
Where does it hurt	nereniz ağrıyor	ner en eez aa ruh yor
I'm not good	iyi değilim	ee deh eel eem
I have a fever	ateşim var	a teh sheem var
I have constant back pain	devamlı sırt ağrım var	dev am luh surt aarum var
I have constant headache	sık sık baş ağrım var	suck suck bash a rum var

Chapters

Learn Turkish In One Week

English	Turkish	Pronunciation
Sometimes I have a stomach ache	bazen midem ağrım var	ba zen mee dem aa rum var
I feel nauseous	midem bulanıyor	mee dem bool an uh yor
How is your sleep	uykunuz nasıl	oy koon ooz na sull
I can't sleep well	iyi uyuyamıyorum	ee oy oo yam uh yor oom
Sometimes	bazen	ba zen
Sometimes I feel dizzy	bazen başım dönüyor	ba zen bash um durn uh yor
How is your appetite	iştahınız nasıl	eesh ta hun uz na sull
I have no appetite for food	yemek için iştahım yok	yeh mek eech in eesh ta hum yok
My feet hurt	ayaklarım ağrıyor	eye ack la rum aa ruh yor
I've got a sore throat	boğazım ağrıyor	boe aa zum aa ruh yor
Blood pressure	tansiyon	tan see yon
Blood pressure normal	tansiyon normal	tan see yon nor mal
Please lie down	lütfen uzanın	lewt fen oo za nun
Breathe deeply	derin nefes alın	deh reen nay fes al un
Cough please	öksürn lütfen	urk surn lewt fen
Does that hurt	acıyor mı	a jee yor muh
Open your mouth	ağzınızı aç	aaz uh nuz uh ach
It's very serious	çok ciddi	chok jee dee
It's not serious	ciddi değil	jee dee deh eel

Chapters

Learn Turkish In One Week

English	Turkish	Pronunciation
What's wrong with you	neyin var	nay een var
What's wrong with you	neyiniz var	nay een iz var
I've got no energy	halsizim	hal seez eem
X-ray	röntgen	rurnt gen
Medicine	ilaç	eel ach
Antibiotic	antibiyotik	an tee bee oh teek
Vaccine	aşı	a shuh
Pain killer	ağrı kesici	aa ruh keh see jee
Abdominal pain	karın ağrısı	ka run aa ruh suh
Back pain	sırt ağrısı	surt aa ruh suh
Bleeding from anywhere	herhangi bir yerden kanama	her han gee bir yer den kan a ma
Bloody stools	kanlı dışkılama	kan luh dush kull ama
Chest pain	göğüs ağrısı	gur urs a ruh suh
Chills	titreme	tee treh meh
Cramps	kramplar	cramp lar
Dark urine	koyu renk idrar	koy oo renk ee drar
Diarrhea	ishal	ee shal
Ear pain	kulak ağrısı	kool ak aa ruh suh
Fever	ateş	a tesh

Chapters

Learn Turkish In One Week

English	Turkish	Pronunciation
Hemorrhoids	basur	ba sur
Itching	kaşınma	kash un ma
Joint pain	eklem ağrısı	eck lem aa ruh suh
Throat pain	boğaz ağrısı	boe az aa ruh suh
Tooth pain	diş ağrısı	deesh aa ruh suh
Vaginal bleeding	vajinal kanama	va shyeen al kan a ma
Vomiting	kusma	koos ma
Pain	ağrı	aa ruh
Infection	enfeksiyon	en fek see yon
Difficulty breathing	nefes almada zorluk	neh fes al ma da zor look
High cholesterol	yüksek kolestorol	yewk sek kol es toh rol
Allergy	alerji	a ler shyee
Depression	depresyon	Deh pres yon
Sadness	üzüntü	ewz oon tew
Seizure	nöbet	nur bet
Insomnia	uykusuzluk	ooy koo sooz look
Blood	kan	kan
Burn	yanık	ya nuk
Clean	temiz	teh meez

Chapters

Learn Turkish In One Week

English	Turkish	Pronunciation
Dead	ölü	ur loo
Injured	yaralı	ya ra luh
Poison	zehir	zeh heer
Sick	hasta	ha sta
Wound	yara	ya ra
I am a doctor	ben doktorum	ben dok tor oom
Are you a doctor	doktor musunuz	dok tor muh soon uz
I am not a doctor	ben doktor değilim	ben dok tor deh eel eem
Bone	kemik	keh meek
Brain	beyin	bay een
Ribs	kaburga	ka boor ga
Skull	kafatası	kaf at a suh
Spine	belkemiği	bell kem ee ee
Surgeon	cerrah	jer ra
Family doctor	aile doktoru	eye leh dok toh roo
Gynecologist	kadın doktoru	ka dun dok toh roo
Psychologist	psikolog	pee see koh log
Dentist	diş hekimi	deesh her kee mee
Pharmacist	eczacı	ej zar juh

Chapters

Learn Turkish In One Week

English	Turkish	Pronunciation
Ambulance	ambulans	am boo lans
Illness	hastalık	ha sta luk
Patient	hasta	ha sta
Treatment	tedavi	ted ah vee
Acne	sivilce	see veel jeh
Anaemia	kansızlık	kan suz luk
Asthma	astım	ass tum
Bandage	bandaj	ban darsh
Blood sample	kan örneği	kan urn eh ee
Blood transfusion	kan nakli	kan nak lee
Bronchitis	bronşit	bron sheet
Cancer	kanser	kan ser
Disabled	engelli	en gel lee
Injection	iğne	ee neh
Operation	ameliyat	a meh lee yat
Scar	yara izi	ya ra ee zee
Stitch	dikiş	dee keesh
Stiches	dikişler	dee keesh ler
Vaccination	aşı	a shuh

Chapters

Learn Turkish In One Week

English	Turkish	Pronunciation
Blister	su toplama	soo top la ma
Chicken pox	suçiçeği	soo chee cheh ee
Cut	kesik	keh seek
Diabetes	şeker hastalığı	sheh ker has ta luh
Dizziness	baş dönmesi	bash durn meh see
Food poisoning	yemek zehirlenmesi	yeh mek zeh heer len meh see
Heart disease	kalp hastalığı	kalp has ta luh
Jaundice	sarılık	sa ruh look
Fatigue	yorgunluk	yor goon look
Lung cancer	akciğer kanseri	ak jee er kan seh ree
Malaria	sıtma	sut ma
Measles	kızamık	kuz a muck
Migraine	migren	mee gren
Miscarriage	düşük yapma	dew sewk yap ma
Typhoid	tifo	tee foe
Mumps	kabakulak	ka ba kool ak
Pneumonia	zatürre	za tew reh
Polio	çocuk felci	choe jook fel jee
Rabies	kuduz	koo dooz

Chapters

Learn Turkish In One Week

English	Turkish	Pronunciation
Rash	kaşıntı	ka shun tuh
Rheumatism	romatizma	roh ma teez ma
Schizophrenia	şizofreni	sheez oh fren ee
Slipped disc	bel fıtığı	bel fuh tuh uh
Sprain	burkulma	bur kool ma
Stroke	felç	felch
Sunburn	güneş yanığı	gewn esh yan uh
Swelling	şişme	sheesh meh
Virus	virüs	vee roos
Wart	siğil	seel
Pill	hap	hap
Pulse	nabız	na buz
Urine sample	idrar örneği	ee drar ur neh ee
Blind	kör	kur
Death	sağır	saa ur
Pregnant	hamile	ha mee leh
To limp	topallamak	top al la mak
To be sick	hasta olmak	has ta ol mak
To recover	iyileşmek	eel esh mek

Chapters

Learn Turkish In One Week

Hotel

English	Turkish	Pronunciation
Do you have any vacant rooms	boş odanız var mı	bosh or dan uz var muh
Are there any free rooms	boş oda var mı	bosh or da var muh
I'd like a room	bir oda istiyorum	bir or da ees tee yor oom
I'd like	istiyorum	ees tee yor oom
I want a single room	tek kişilik bir oda istiyorum	tek kee shee leek bir or da ees tee yor oom
I want a double room	çift kişilik bir oda istiyorum	cheeft kee shee leek bir or da ee stee yor oom
Please	lütfen	lewt fen
My name is ...	benim adım	ben eem a dum
Surname	soyadı	soy a duh
First floor	birinci kak	bee reen jee cat
Second floor	ikinci kat	eek een jee cat
Third floor	üçüncü kat	ooch oon jew cat
Tenth floor	onuncu kat	on oon joo cat
Twin bed	ikiz yatak	ee keez ya tak
Bed	yatak	ya tak
Single bed	tek kişilik yatak	tek kee shee leek ya tak
Double bed	çift kişilik yatak	cheeft kee shee leek ya tak

Chapters

Learn Turkish In One Week

English	Turkish	Pronunciation
Pillow	yastık	yas tuk
I need another pillow	başka bir yastığa ihtiyacım var	bash ka bir yas ta ee tee yaa jum var
Are there any more pillows	başka yastık var mı	bash ka yas tuk var muh
Towel	havlu	hav loo
Soap	sabun	sa boon
Ice	buz	booz
Swimming pool	yüzme havuzu	yewz meh hav oo zoo
With a shower	duşlu	doosh loo
A room with a shower	duşlu bir oda	doosh loo bir or da
Shower	duş	doosh
View	manzara	man za ra
With a view	manzaralı	man za ra luh
A room with a view	manzaralı bir oda	man za ra luh bir or da
Balcony	balkon	bal con
With a balcony	balkonlu	bal con loo
A room with a balcony	balkonlu oda	bal con loo or da
Facing the sea	denize bakan	den eez eh ba kan
A room facing the sea	denize bakan bir oda	den eez eh ba kan bir or da

Chapters

Learn Turkish In One Week

English	Turkish	Pronunciation
What time is breakfast?	kahvaltı ne zaman	karv al tuh neh za man
Breakfast	kahvaltı	karv al tuh
How much is	ne kadar	neh ka dar
How much is it for bed and breakfast?	yatak ve kahvaltı ne kadar	ya tak veh karv al tuh neh ka dar
Is everything included?	her şey dahil mi	her shay da heel mee
That's too expensive	çok pahalı	chok pa ha luh
That's too much	çok fazla	chok faz la
Small	küçük	Kew chewk
Noisy	gürültülü	goo rool too lew
Dark	karanlık	ka ran luk
Hot	sıcak	suh jak
Cold	soğuk	soh ook
This room is too ...	bu oda çok	boo or da chok
This room is too big	bu oda çok küçük	boo or da chok cew chewk
This room is too hot	bu oda çok sıcak	boo or da chok suh jak
Can you fill this form in please	bu formu doldurur musunuz lütfen	boo for moo dol doo roor moo soon uz lewt fen
Sign here please	burayı imzalayın lütfen	boo reye uh eem zar leye un lewt fen

Chapters

Learn Turkish In One Week

English	Turkish	Pronunciation
First name	adı	a duh
Surname	soyadı	soy a duh
Nationality	uyruğu	oy roo oo
Marital status	medeni durumu	meh den ee doo rum oo
Single	bekâr	beh kar
Married	evli	ev lee
Date of birth	doğum tarihi	doe oom tar ee hee
Place of birth	doğum yeri	doe oom yeh ree
Profession / job	mesleği	mes leh ee
Place of residence	ikametgâh	ee kam et ga
Passport please	pasaport lütfen	pas a port lewt fen
Your passport please	pasaportunuz lütfen	pas a port un uz lewt fen
My key please	anahtarım lütfen	an a ta rum lewt fen
I've lost my key	anahtarımı kaybettim	an a ta rum uh keye bay teem
Another towel	başka havlu	bash ka hav loo
Blanket	battaniye	bat an ee yeh
Hanger	askı	ask uh
Newspaper	gazete	ga zeh teh
Can you clean the room	odayı temizler misiniz	or deye uh tem eez ler mee seen iz

Chapters

Learn Turkish In One Week

English	Turkish	Pronunciation
I'd like to speak with the manager	müdürle konuşmak istiyorum	mew dur leh kon oosh mak ee stee yor oom
The shower doesn't work	duş çalışmıyor	doosh chal ush muh yor
Doesn't work	çalışmıyor	chal ush muh yor
Tap	musluk	moos look
Air conditioning	klima	klee ma
Television	televizyon	teh leh veez yon
Lamp	lamba	lam ba
Socket	priz	pee reez
Telephone	telefon	teh leh fon
There is no light in my room	odamda ışık yok	or dam da uh shuk yoe k
The fuse has blown	sigorta atmış	see gor ta at mush
The toilet is blocked	tuvalet tıkalı	too va let tuk a luh
The toilet won't flush	tuvalet tıkalı	too va let tuk a luh
The tap drips	musluk damlıyor	moos look dam luh yor
What is your room number?	oda numaranız kaç	or da noo ma ran uz cach
What time is breakfast	kahvaltı saat kaç	karv al tuh sart cach
Breakfast is at eight	kahvaltı sekizde	karv al tuh seh keez deh

Chapters

Learn Turkish In One Week

English	Turkish	Pronunciation
I want breakfast	kahvaltı istiyorum	karv al tuh ee stee yor oom
Can I have breakfast in my room	odamda kahvaltı yapabilir miyim	or dam da karv al tuh yap a beel ir meem
How do you like your eggs?	yumurtanızı nasıl istersiniz	yoo mur tan uz uh na sul ee ster seen iz
Hard boiled	katı	ka tuh
Soft boiled egg	rafadan yumurta	ra fa dan yoo moor ta
Is my bill ready?	hesabım hazır mı	heh sa bum ha zur muh
Bulb	ampul	am pool
Key	anahtar	a na tar
Bathroom	banyo	ban yoe
Five star hotel	beş yıldızlı otel	besh yul duz luh oe tel
Bedsheet	çarşaf	char shaf
Exit	çıkış	chuk ush
Entrance	giriş	gee reesh
Deposit	depozito	deh poh zee toe
Price	fiyat	fee yat
Porter	hamal	ha mal
Toilet paper	tuvalet kağıdı	too va let car uh duh

Chapters

Learn Turkish In One Week

Istanbul

Istanbul used to be called Byzantium and Constantinople and is the largest city in Turkey and also the country's economic, cultural and historic centre. Istanbul is the only city in the world to be divided by two continents. One part lies in Europe and the other in Asia.

Speaking from experience, Istanbul is a fabulous city to visit and compared to other major cities, relatively cheap. The people are very friendly and the mosques and other attractions are awesome. The city is easy to get around and there is always a cafe or restaurant welcoming you for a pit stop before continuing with your adventure.

Istanbul's Asian part is separated by the Bosphorus Strait, a 31 km long waterway that connects the black Sea with the Sea of Marmara. There are a couple of suspension bridges connecting the two continents together.

The Asian side is more relaxed with fewer hotels and tourist attractions. A great place to get refreshments and sit back and watch the world go by. The European side is a lot more busy with plenty of tourist attractions and the city's main commercial centre with banks, shops and corporations. The majority of Istanbuls population live in this section.

Tourist attractions not to miss include,The blue Mosque, Hagia Sophia, Topkapi Palace, Grand Bazaar, crossing the Bosphorus Strait, Basilica Cistern, Galata Tower, Dolmabahçe Palace and Suleymaniye Mosque.

Chapters

Learn Turkish In One Week

House

English	Turkish	Pronunciation
House	ev	ev
In the house	evde	ev deh
She's in the house	o evde	oe ev deh
Garden	bahçe	ba cheh
In the garden	bahçede	ba cheh deh
He's in the garden	o bahçede	oe ba cheh deh
Kitchen	mutfak	moot fak
In the kitchen	mutfakta	moot fak ta
She's in the kitchen	o mutfakta	oe moot fak ta
Window	pencere	pen jeh reh
Chimney	baca	ba ja
Apartment	apartman	a part man
Balcony	balkon	bal kon
Bathroom	banyo	ban yoe
First floor	birinci kat	bee reen jee cat
Second floor	ikinci kat	ee keen jee cat
Third floor	üçüncü kat	ooch oon jew cat
Fourth floor	dördüncü kat	dur doon jew cat
Fifth floor	beşinci kat	besh een jee cat

Chapters

Learn Turkish In One Week

English	Turkish	Pronunciation
Roof	çatı	cha tuh
Fence	çit	cheet
Wall	duvar	doo var
Garage	garaj	ga rarsh
Entrance	giriş	gee reesh
Hall	hol	hol
Door	kapı	ka pu
Open the door	kapıyı aç	ka pu yuh ach
Close the door	kapıyı kapat	ka pu yuh ka pat
Come in	içeri gir	ee cheh ree geer
Doorbell	kapı zili	ka puh zee lee
Floor	kat	kat
Corridor	koridor	koh ree dor
Hut	kulübe	kuh loo beh
Letter box	mektup kutusu	mek toop koo too soo
Stairs	merdivenler	mer dee ven ler
Guest room	misafir odası	mee sa feer or da suh
Room	oda	or da
Sitting room	oturma odası	oh toor ma or da suh

Chapters

Learn Turkish In One Week

English	Turkish	Pronunciation
Porch	sundurma	soon dur ma
Ceiling	tavan	ta van
Terrace	teras	teh ras
Brick	tuğla	too la
Toilet	tuvalet	too va let
Top floor	üst kat	oost cat
Villa	villa	vee la
Bed room	yatak odası	ya tak or da suh
Dining room	yemek odası	yeh mek or da suh
Basement	zemin kat	zay meen kat
Chandelier	avize	a vee zeh
Clock	saat	sart
Carpet	halı	ha luh
Book	kitap	kee tap
Bookshelf	kitaplık	kee tap luk
Chair	sandalye	san dal yeh
Armchair	koltuk	kol took
Ash tray	kül tablası	kewl tab luh suh
Table	masa	ma sa

Chapters

Learn Turkish In One Week

English	Turkish	Pronunciation
Cushion	minder	meen der
Sitting room	oturma odası	oh tur ma or da suh
Curtains	perdeler	per deh ler
Curtain	perde	per deh
Radio	radyo	rad yoe
Coffee table	sehpa	seh pa
Fire place	şömine	shur mee neh
Telephone	telefon	teh leh fon
Vase	vazo	va zoe
Blanket	battaniye	ba tan ee yeh
Alarm clock	çalar saat	cha lar sart
Sheet	çarşaf	char shaf
Bed sheet	çarşaf	char shaf
Coat hanger	elbise askısı	el bee seh ask uh suh
Wardrobe	gardırop	gar duh rop
Bedside table	komidin	kom ee deen
Chest of drawers	konsol	kon sol
Dressing table	tuvalet masası	too va let ma sa suh
Pillow	yastık	yas tuk

Chapters

Learn Turkish In One Week

English	Turkish	Pronunciation
Bed	yatak	ya tak
Quilt	yorgan	yor gan
Knife	bıçak	buh chak
Fork	çatal	cha tal
Spoon	kaşık	ka shuk
Tea spoon	çay kaşığı	cheye ca shuh
Tablespoon	yemek çay kaşığı	yeh mek ca shuh
Pepperpot	biberlik	bee ber leek
Dish washer	bulaşık makinesi	bool la shuk ma keen eh see
Refrigerator	buzdolabı	booz doh la buh
Coffe pot	cezve	jez veh
Glass	bardak	bar dak
Tea glass	çay bardağı	cheye bar da uh
Wine glass	şarap bardağı	sha rap bar da uh
Teapot	çaydanlık	cheye dan luk
Waste bin	çöp sepeti	chop seh peh tee
Deep freeze	derin dondurucu	deh reen don dur roo joo
Cupboard	dolap	dol ap
Bread bin	ekmeklik	ek mek leek

Chapters

Learn Turkish In One Week

English	Turkish	Pronunciation
Sink	lavabo	lav a boe
Oven	fırın	fuh run
Bowl	kâse	ka seh
Plate	tabak	ta bak
Cup	fincan	feen jan
Mug	maşrapa	mash ra pa
Jar	kavanoz	kav a noz
Ladle	kepçe	kep cheh
Tongs	maşa	ma sha
Mixer	mikser	meek ser
Jug	sürahi	sur aa hee
Sugar	şeker	sheh ker
Sugar bowl	şekerlik	sheh ker leek
Bottle opener	şişe açacağı	shee sheh a cha ja uh
Saucepan	tencere	ten jeh reh
Tray	tepsi	tep see
Toaster	tost makinası	tost ma keen a suh
Salt shaker	tuzluk	tooz look
Salt	tuz	tooz

Chapters

Learn Turkish In One Week

English	Turkish	Pronunciation
Egg	yumurta	yoo moor ta
Eggcup	yumurtalık	yoo moor ta luk
Mirror	ayna	eye na
Tooth	diş	deesh
Toothbrush	diş fırçası	deesh fur cha suh
Toothpaste	diş macunu	deesh ma joon oo
Do you have toothpaste?	diş macunun var mı	deesh ma joon oo var muh
Shower	duş	doosh
Tile	fayans	feye ans
Towel	havlu	hav loo
There's no towel	havlu yok	hav loo yoe k
Bath	küvet	kew vet
Washbasin	lavabo	lav a boe
Tap	musluk	moos look
Soap	sabun	sa boon
Hair	saç	sach
Hairbrush	saç fırçası	sach fur cha suh
Sponge	sünger	soon ger
Shampoo	şampuan	sham poo an

Chapters

Learn Turkish In One Week

English	Turkish	Pronunciation
Comb	tarak	ta rak
Shaving brush	tıraş fırçası	tuh rash fur cha suh
Shaving cream	tıraş kremi	tuh rash krem ee
Electric razor	tıraş makinesi	tuh rash ma keen eh see
Shaving soap	tıraş sabunu	tuh rash sa boon oo
Toilet	tuvalet	too va let
Water	su	soo
Hot water	sıcak su	suh jack soo
There's no hot water	sıcak su yok	suh jack soo yoe k
Cold water	soğuk su	so ook soo
The water is cold	su soğuk	soo so ook
Toilet paper	tuvalet kağıdı	too va let ka uh duh
Washing machine	çamaşır makinesi	cham a shur ma keen eh see
Sewing machine	dikiş makinesi	dee keesh ma keen eh see
Vacuum cleaner	elektrik süpürgesi	eh lek treek sew pew geh see
Hair dryer	saç kurutma makinesi	sach coo root ma ma keen eh see
Iron	ütü	oo too
Computer	bilgisayar	beel gee seye ar
Light	ışık	uh shuck

Chapters

Learn Turkish In One Week

English	Turkish	Pronunciation
Tweezers	cımbız	jum buz
Safety pin	çengelli iğne	chen geh lee ee neh
Hand cream	el kremi	el krem ee
Eye shadow	far	far
Brush	fırça	fur cha
Foundation	fondöten	fon dur ten
Night cream	gece kremi	geh jeh krem ee
Eye pencil	göz kalemi	gurz ka lem ee
Sun cream	güneş kremi	gewn esh krem ee
Cream	krem	krem
Sun oil	güneş yağı	gewn esh yaa uh
Moisturizer	nemlendirici	nem len dee ree jee
Perfume	parfüm	par fewm
Mascara	rimel	ree mel
Lipstick	ruj	roosh
Pen	kalem	ka lem
Hair cream	saç kremi	sach krem ee
Battery	pil	peel
Candle	mum	moom

Chapters

Learn Turkish In One Week

English	Turkish	Pronunciation
Matches	kibritler	kee breet ler
Hair spray	saç spreyi	sach spray ee
Sponge	sünger	soon ger
Shampoo	şampuan	Sham poo an
Talcum powder	talk pudrası	talc poo dra suh
Tampon	tampon	tam pon
Shaving brush	tıraş fırçası	tuh rash fur cha suh
Shaving cream	tıraş kremi	tuh rash krem ee
Shaving soap	tıraş sabunu	tuh rash sa bun oo
Nail clippers	tırnak makası	tur nak ma ka suh
Nail file	tırnak törpüsü	tur nak tur poo soo
Face	yüz	yewz
Facecloth	yüz havlusu	yewz hav loo soo
Face powder	yüz pudrası	yewz poo dra suh
Key	anahtar	an ah tar
Piano	piyano	pee yan oe
Fire	ateş	a tesh
Wig	peruk	peh rook
Air conditioning	klima	klee ma

Chapters

Learn Turkish In One Week

Market / Supermarket

English	Turkish	Pronunciation
Bread	ekmek	ek mek
Egg	yumurta	yoo moor ta
Cheese	peynir	pay neer
Flour	un	oon
Detergent	deterjan	deh ter shyan
Rice	pirinç	pee reench
Tomato paste	salça	sal cha
Macaroni	makarna	ma kar na
Butter	tereyağı	teh reh yar uh
Margarine	margarin	mar ga reen
Milk	süt	sewt
How much is this?	bu ne kadar	boo neh ka dar
How much is that?	şu ne kadar	shoo neh ka dar
Very expensive	çok pahalı	chok pa ha luh
That's cheap	bu ucuz	boo oo jooz
That's too expensive	bu çok pahalı	boo chok pa ha luh
I want	istiyorum	ee stee yor oom
Two please	iki lütfen	ee kee lewt fen
One more please	bir tane daha, lütfen	bir tar neh da ha lewt fen

Chapters

Learn Turkish In One Week

English	Turkish	Pronunciation
I want a kilo	bir kilo istiyorum	bir kee loe is tee yor oom
I want two kilos	iki kilo istiyorum	ee kee kee loe is tee yor oom
That's all thanks	hepsi bu kadar, teşekkürler	hep see boo ka dar tesh eh kew ler
How much?	ne kadar	Neh ka dar
How much?	kaç para	cach pa ra
Money	para	pa ra
Here you are	buyrun	boy roon
Bag	poşet	posh et
Do you have a bag?	poşet var mı	posh et var muh
How much is coffee?	kahve ne kadar	ka veh neh ka dar
Where's the sugar?	şeker nerede	shay ker neh reh deh
Where's the milk?	süt nerede	sewt neh reh deh
Fresh bread	taze ekmek	tar zeh ek mek
Is there?	var mı	var muh
Are there olives?	zeytin var mı	zay teen var muh
Manager	yönetici	yur neh tee jee
Boss	patron	pa tron
Big boss	büyük patron	boo yewk pa tron
Where's the boss?	patron nerede	pa tron neh reh deh

Chapters

Learn Turkish In One Week

Miscellaneous

English	Turkish	Pronunciation
Shapes	şekiller	sheh keel ler
Circle	daire	deye reh
Square	kare	ka reh
Rectangle	dikdörtgen	deek durt gen
Cone	koni	kon ee
Triangle	üçgen	ooch gen
Cylinder	silindir	see leen deer
Pyramid	piramit	pee ra meet
Curve	eğri	eh ree
Centre	merkez	mer kez
Line	çizgi	cheez gee
Straight line	düz çizgi	dooz cheez gee
Machines and tools	makineler ve aletler	ma keen eh ler veh al et ler
Tool	alet	aa let
Tool box	alet kutusu	aa let koo too soo
Spade	kürek	kew rek
Axe	balta	bal ta
Knife	bıçak	buh chak
Penknife	çakı	chak uh

Chapters

Learn Turkish In One Week

English	Turkish	Pronunciation
Scissors	makas	ma kas
Hammer	çekiç	cheh keech
Nail	çivi	chee vee
Hacksaw	demir testeresi	dem ir tes ter eh see
Brush	fırça	fur cha
Rope	halat	ha lat
Needle	iğne	ee neh
Cotton	pamuk	pam ook
Thread	iplik	eep leek
Pickaxe	kazma	kaz ma
Pliers	kerpeten	ker per ten
Chisel	keski	kes kee
Lock	kilit	keel eet
Drill	matkap	mat cap
Vice	mengene	men geh neh
Ladder	merdiven	mer dee ven
Plane	planya	pee lan ya
Spanner	somun anahtar	som oon an a tar
Wire	tel	tel

Chapters

Learn Turkish In One Week

English	Turkish	Pronunciation
Wire brush	tel fırça	tel fur cha
Saw	testere	tes teh reh
Mallet	tokmak	tok mak
Screw	vida	vee da
Screwdriver	tornavida	tor na vee da
Glue	tutkal	toot kal
Flowers	çiçekler	chee cek ler
Rose	gül	gool
Tulip	lale	la leh
Daisy	papatya	pa pa tee ya
Carnation	karanfil	ka ran feel
Daffodil	nergis	ner gees
Hyacinth	sümbül	sewm bool
Violet	menekşe	men ek shay
Waterlily	nilüfer	nee loo fer
Continents	kıtalar	cuh ta lar
Africa	Afrika	a free ka
Antarctica	Antarktika	an tark tee ka
Asia	Asya	as ya

Chapters

Learn Turkish In One Week

English	Turkish	Pronunciation
Europe	Avrupa	av roo pa
South America	Güney Amerika	goo nay a meh ree ka
North America	Kuzey Amerika	coo zay a meh ree ka
Australia	Avustralya	a voo stral ya
Earth	dünya	doon ya
Sky	gökyüzü	gurk yoo zoo
Moon	ay	eye
Universe	evren	ev ren
Planet	gezegen	gez eh gen
Space	uzay	ooz eye
Star	yıldız	yull duz
Milky Way	samanyolu	sa man yol oo
Galaxy	galaksi	gal ak see
North Pole	kuzey kutbu	coo zay coot boo
South Pole	güney kutbu	goo nay coot boo
Signs	işaretler	ee shar et ler
Open	açık	a chuk
Closed	kapalı	ka pa luh
Waiting room	bekleme salonu	bek lem eh sal on oo

Chapters

Learn Turkish In One Week

English	Turkish	Pronunciation
No waiting	beklemek yasaktir	bek leh mek ya sak tir
Rooms available	boş oda var	bosh or da var
No rooms	oda yok	or da yok
No free rooms	boş oda yok	bosh or da yok
Vacant	boş	bosh
Men	erkek / erkekler	er kek / er kek ler
Mr	bay	beye
Gentlemen	beyler / bayler	bay ler / beye ler
Mrs	bayan	beye an
Woman	kadın	ka dun
Ladies	bayanlar	beye an lar
Pull	çekiniz	check een iz
Entrance	giriş	gee reesh
Exit	çıkış	chuh kush
Caution	dikkat	deek kat
Stop	dur	dur
Do not touch	dokunmayınız	dok oon may un uz
Not drinkable	içilemez	eech ee leh mez
Push	itiniz	ee teen eez

Chapters

Learn Turkish In One Week

English	Turkish	Pronunciation
For rent	kiralık	kir a luk
For sale	satılık	sat uh luk
Beware of the dog	dikkat köpek var	dee cat kur pek var
Private	özel	ur zel
No parking	park yapılmaz	park ya pul maz
Hot	sıcak	suh jak
No smoking	sigara içilmez	see gar a eech eel mez
Cold	soğuk	soe ook
Parking	park yeri	park yeh ree
Danger	tehlike	teh lee keh
Reserved	tutulmuş	toot ool moosh
Toilet	tuvalet	too va let
Arrival	varış	va rush
Departures	gidiş	geed eesh
Forbidden	yasaktır	ya sak tur
Stationery	kırtasiye	kur ta see yeh
Pen	kalem	ka lem
Pencil	kurşun kalem	kur shoon ka lem
Pencil sharpener	kalemtıraş	ka lem tuh rash

Chapters

Learn Turkish In One Week

English	Turkish	Pronunciation
Paper	kağıt	kaa ut
Paper clip	ataç	a tach
Ordinals	sıra sayıları	suh ra seye uh la ruh
First	birinci	bee reen jee
Second	ikinci	ee keen jee
Third	üçüncü	ooch oon joo
Fourth	dördüncü	dur ewn joo
Fifth	beşinci	besh een jee
Sixth	altıncı	alt un juh
Seventh	yedinci	yed een jee
Eighth	sekizinci	seh keez een jee
Nineth	dokuzuncu	doh kooz oon joo
Tenth	onuncu	on oon joo
Eleventh	on birinci	on bee reen jee
Twelth	onikinci	on ee keen jee
Thirteenth	on üçüncü	on ooch oon joo
Fourteenth	on dördüncü	on dur doon joo
Fifteenth	on beşinci	on besh een jee
Sixteenth	on altıncı	on alt un juh

Chapters

Learn Turkish In One Week

English	Turkish	Pronunciation
Seventeenth	on yedinci	on yed een jee
Eighteenth	on sekizinci	on seh keez een jee
Nineteenth	on dokuzuncu	on doh cooz oon joo
Twentieth	yirminci	yeer meen jee
Twenty-first	yirmi birinci	yeer mee bir een jee
Nature	doğa	doe a
Island	ada	a da
On the island	adada	a da da
Iceberg	buzdağı	booz da uh
Glacier	buzul	boo zool
Desert	çöl	churl
Mountain	dağ	daa
Sea	deniz	den eez
Lake	göl	gurl
River	nehir	neh hir
Canal	kanal	ka nal
Continent	kıta	kuh ta
Coast	kıyı	kuh yuh
Forest	orman	or man

Chapters

Learn Turkish In One Week

English	Turkish	Pronunciation
Waterfall	şelale	shell a leh
Ocean	okyanus	oe k yan us
Hill	tepe	teh peh
Valley	vadi	var dee
Volcano	yanardağ	yan ar daa
Music	müzik	mew zeek
Harp	arp	arp
Drum	davul	da vool
Cello	çello	chay loe
Flute	flüt	floot
Guitar	gitar	gee tar
Violin	keman	keh man
Clarinet	klarnet	clar net
Oboe	obua	oe boo a
Piano	piyano	pee yan oe
Sports	spor	spor
Football	futbol	foot bol
Horse racing	at yarışı	at ya ruh shuh
Shooting	atıcılık	a tuh juh luk

Chapters

Learn Turkish In One Week

English	Turkish	Pronunciation
Fishing	balıkçılık	ba luk chuh luk
Fencing	eskrim	esk reem
Basketball	basketbol	bas ket bol
Baseball	beyzbol	bayz bol
Hunting	avcılık	av jul luk
Car racing	araba yarışı	a ra ba yar uh shuh
Gymnastics	jimnastik	shyeem nas teek
Running	koşu	koh shoo
Rowing	kürek	koo rek
Table tennis	masa tenisi	ma sa ten ee see
Archery	okçuluk	ock choo look
Tennis	tenis	ten eece
Swimming	yüzme	yewz may
Traffic	trafik	tra feek
Avenue	bulvar	bool var
Street	sokak	soe kak
Street	cadde	ja deh
Crossing	geçit	geh cheet
Speed	hız	huz

Chapters

Learn Turkish In One Week

English	Turkish	Pronunciation
Fast	hızlı	huz luh
Slow	yavaş	ya vash
The car is going vey fast	araba çok hızlı gidiyor	a ra ba chok huz luh gee dee yor
That car is going very fast	o araba çok hızlı gidiyor	oe a ra ba chok huz luh gee dee yor
Motorway	otoyol	oh toe yol
Road	yol	yol
Accident	kaza	ka za
Red light	kırmızı ışık	kur muh zuh uh shuk
Green light	yeşil ışık	yeh sheel uh shuk
Traffic lights	trafik ışıkları	tra feek uh shuk la ruh
Yellow / amber light	sarı ışık	sa ruh uh shuk
Parking	park yeri	park yeh ree
Tunnel	tünel	tew nel
Pedestrian	yaya	ya ya
Direction	yön	yurn
Pavement	kaldırım	kal duh rum
Ship	gemi	geh mee
Island	ada	a da

Chapters

Learn Turkish In One Week

English	Turkish	Pronunciation
Main deck	ana güverte	an a goo ver teh
Flag	bayrak	beye rack
First class	birinci mevki	bee reen jee mev kee
Second class	ikinci mevki	ee keen jee mev kee
Lifebuoy	can simidi	jan see mee dee
Life jacket	can yeleği	jan yel eh ee
Wave	dalga	dal ga
Sea	deniz	den eez
Lighthouse	deniz feneri	den eez fen eh ree
Ship wreck	deniz kazası	den eez kaz a suh
Sailor	denizci	den eez jee
Outside cabin	dış kamara	dush kam a ra
Seasickness	deniz tutulması	den eez too tool ma suh
Inside cabin	iç kamara	eech kam a ra
Deck	güverte	goo ver teh
Steward	kamarot	kam a rot
Captain	kaptan	kap tan
Coast	kıyı	kuh yuh
Air conditioning	klima	klee ma

Chapters

Learn Turkish In One Week

English	Turkish	Pronunciation
Bridge	köprü	kur proo
Crew	mürettebat	mur eh teh bat
Sick bay	revir	rev ir
Shallow water	sığ su	suh soo
Deckchair	şezlong	shez long
Upper deck	üst güverte	oost goo ver teh
Passenger	yolcu	yol joo
Passenger ship	yolcu gemisi	yol joo geh mee see
Blanket	battaniye	ba tan ee yeh
Bedsheet	çarşaf	char shaf
Window	pencere	pen jeh reh
Lights	ışıklar	uh shuk lar
Curtain	perde	per deh
Complaint	şikayet	shee keye yet
Iron	ütü	oo too
Arrival	varış	va rush
Departure	kalkış	kal kush
Pillow	yastık	yas tuk
Submarine	denizaltı	den eez al tuh

Chapters

Learn Turkish In One Week

English	Turkish	Pronunciation
Boat	kayık	keye uck
Boat	tekne	tek neh
Yacht	yat	yat
Sailing boat	yelkenli	yel ken lee
Raft	sal	sal
Vehicles	araçlar	a rach lar
Car	araba	a ra ba
Lorry	kamyon	kam yon
Ambulance	ambulans	am boo lans
Vehicle	araç	a rach
Aircraft	uçak	oo chak
Spaceship	uzay gemisi	oo zeye gem ee see
Taxi	taksi	tak see
Van	kamyonet	kam yon et
Jeep	jip	jeep
Balloon	balon	ba lon
Bicycle	bisiklet	bee see clet
Cable car	teleferik	tel eh feh reek
Tren	tren	tren

Chapters

Learn Turkish In One Week

English	Turkish	Pronunciation
Tram	tramvay	tram veye
Tractor	traktör	trak tur
Bus	otobüs	oh toe boo s
Firetruck	itfaiye arabası	eet feye yeh a ra buh suh
Office	büro	boo roe
Diary	ajanda	a shyan da
Ruler	cetvel	jet vel
Paper	kağıt	kaa ut
Pen	kalem	ka lem
Envelope	zarf	zarf
Boss	patron	pa tron
Glue	zamk	zamk
Ink	mürekkep	moo rek kep
Printer	yazıcı	yaz uh juh
Typewriter	daktilo	dak tee loe
Computer	bilgisayar	beel gee seye ar
Calendar	takvim	tak veem
Accessories	aksesuarlar	ak seh soo ar lar
Wedding ring	alyans	al yans

Chapters

Learn Turkish In One Week

English	Turkish	Pronunciation
Comb	tarak	ta rak
Bracelet	bilezik	beel eh zeek
Headscarf	başörtüsü	bash ur too soo
Purse	cüzdan	joos dan
Wallet	cüzdan	joos dan
Scarf	eşarp	eh sharp
Scarf	kaşkol	kash kol
Bag	çanta	chan ta
Bag	poşet	posh et
Handbag	çantası	chan ta suh
Glasses	gözlük	gurz look
Lighter	çakmak	chak mak
Matches	kibritler	kee breet ler
Belt	kemer	keh mer
Hat	şapka	shap ka
Earring	küpe	koo pay
Handkerchief	mendil	men deel
Ring	yüzük	yoo zook
Hairpin	saç tokası	sach tok a suh

Chapters

Learn Turkish In One Week

English	Turkish	Pronunciation
Brush	fırça	fur cha
Tweezers	cımbız	jum buz
Nail polish remover	aseton	ass eh ton
Safety pin	çengelli iğne	chen gel lee een ay
Hand cream	el kremi	el crem ee
Hand lotion	el losyonu	el loss yon oo
Nail polish	oje	oe shyeh
Perfume	parfüm	par foom
Moisturizer	nemlendirici	nem len dee ree jee
Eye pencil	göz kalemi	gurz ka lem ee
Eye shadow	far	far
Powder	pudra	poo dra
Mascara	rimel	ree mel
Lipstick	ruj	roo sh
Nail file	tırnak törpüsü	tur nak tur poo soo
Nail clippers	tırnak makası	tur nak mak a suh
Tampons	tamponlar	tam pon lar
Sponge	sünger	soon ger
Face powder	yüz pudrası	yewz poo dra suh

Chapters

Learn Turkish In One Week

English	Turkish	Pronunciation
Hair spray	saç spreyi	sach spray ee
Face cloth	yüz havlusu	yewz hav loo soo
Shaving brush	traş fırçası	trash fur cha suh
Shaving cream	tıraş kremi	trash crem ee
Shaving soap	tıraş sabunu	trash sa boo noo
Talcum powder	talk pudrası	tal k poo dra suh
Human Being	insan oğlu	een san oe loo
Man	adam	a dam
Man	erkek	er kek
Male	erkek	er kek
Mr	bay	beye
Boy	oğlan	oe lan
Boy	erkek çocuk	er kek choe jook
Woman	kadın	ka dun
Female	kadın	ka dun
Mrs	bayan	beye an
Girl	kız	kuz
Sex / gender	cinsiyet	jeen see yet
Men	erkekler	er kek ler

Chapters

Learn Turkish In One Week

English	Turkish	Pronunciation
Race	ırk	urk
Humanity	insanlık	een san luk
Person	kişi	kee shee
Name	isim	ee seem
Miss	bayan	beye an
Signature	imza	eem za
Maiden name	kızlık soyadı	kuz luk soy a duh
Surname	soyadı	soy a duh
Nickname	takma ad	tak ma ad
Age	yaş	yash
Child	çocuk	choe jook
Baby	bebek	beh bek
Young	genç	gench
Old	eski	es kee
Adult	yetişkin	yeh teesh keen
Middle-aged	orta yaşlı	or ta yash luh
Newly born	yeni doğmuş	yeh nee doe moosh
Birthday	doğum günü	doe oom goo noo
Life	hayat	heye at

Chapters

Learn Turkish In One Week

English	Turkish	Pronunciation
Death	ölüm	oe lewm
Birth	doğum	doe oom
Body	beden	beh den
Corpse	ceset	jeh set
Grave	mezar	meh zar
Dead	ölü	oe loo
Cemetery	mezarlık	meh zar luk
Suicide	intihar	een tee har
Funeral	cenaze	jen ar zeh
Inheritance	miras	mee ras
Verbs	fiiller	fee ee ler
To make	yapmak	yap mak
To do	yapmak	yap mak
To be hungry	acıkmak	a juk mak
To open	açmak	ach mak
To hurry	acele etmek	a jel eh et mek
To forgive	affetmek	a fet mek
To cry	ağlamak	aa la mak
To take	almak	al mak

Chapters

Learn Turkish In One Week

English	Turkish	Pronunciation
To understand	anlamak	an la mak
To fall in love	aşık olmak	a shuk ol mak
To jump	atlamak	at la mak
To throw	atmak	at mak
To shout	bağırmak	bar ur mak
To leave	ayrılmak	eye rul mak
To tie	bağlamak	bar la mak
To start	başlamak	bash la mak
To sink	batmak	bat mak
To wait	beklemek	bek leh mek
To know	bilmek	beel mek
To paint	boyamak	boy a mak
To empty	boşaltmak	bosh alt mak
To find	bulmak	bool mak
To grow	büyümek	boo yew mek
To call	çağırmak	char ur mak
To work	çalışmak	chal ush mak
To steal	çalmak	chal mak
To pull	çekmek	chek mek

Chapters

Learn Turkish In One Week

English	Turkish	Pronunciation
To draw	çizmek	cheez mek
To dance	dans etmek	dans et mek
To try	denemek	den eh mek
To sew	dikmek	deek mek
To wish	dilemek	deel eh mek
To listen	dinlemek	deen leh mek
To rest	dinlenmek	deen len mek
To touch	dokunmak	doh koon mak
To fill	doldurmak	dol dur mak
To pour	dökmek	durk mek
To turn	dönmek	durn mek
To pray	dua etmek	doo a et mek
To stop	durmak	dur mak
To drop	düşürmek	doo shur mek
To suck	emmek	em mek
To marry	evlenmek	ev len mek
To whisper	fısıldamak	fus ul da mak
To come	gelmek	gel mek
To pass	geçmek	gech mek

Chapters

Learn Turkish In One Week

English	Turkish	Pronunciation
To go	gitmek	geet mek
To dress	giyinmek	gee yeen mek
To bury	gömmek	gurm mek
To send	göndermek	gurn der mek
To see	görmek	gur mek
To interview	görüşmek	gur rewsh mek
To show	göstermek	gur ster mek
To laugh	gülmek	gool mek
To drink	içmek	eech mek
To smoke	sigara içmek	see gar a eech mek
To sign	imzalamak	eem zal a mak
To want	istemek	ee steh mek
To believe	inanmak	een an mak
To push	itmek	eet mek
To get up	kalkmak	kalk mak
To bleed	kanamak	kan a mak
To grab	kapmak	kap mak
To join	katılmak	kat ul mak
To fold	katlamak	kat la mak

Chapters

Learn Turkish In One Week

English	Turkish	Pronunciation
To lose	kaybetmek	keye bet mek
To win	kazanmak	kaz an mak
To cut	kesmek	kes mek
To break	kırmak	kur mak
To lock	kilitlemek	kee leet leh mek
To hire / rent	kiralamak	kee ral a mak
To smell	kokmak	kok mak
To speak	konuşmak	con ush mak
To run	koşmak	kosh mak
To protect	korumak	kor oo mak
To chase	kovalamak	kov al a mak
To read	okumak	oh coo mak
To sit	oturmak	oh tur mak
To play	oynamak	oy na mak
To learn	öğrenmek	ur ren mek
To measure	ölçmek	urlch mek
To kill	öldürmek	url dur mek
To die	ölmek	url mek
To kiss	öpmek	urp mek

Chapters

Learn Turkish In One Week

English	Turkish	Pronunciation
To knit	örmek	ur mek
To miss	özlemek	urz leh mek
To apologise	özür dilemek	ur zur dee leh mek
To polish	parlatmak	par lat mak
To cook	pişirmek	pee shir mek
To hide	saklamak	sak la mak
To shake	sallamak	sal la mak
To buy	satın almak	sa tun al mak
To sell	satmak	sat mak
To choose	seçmek	sech mek
To love	sevmek	sev mek
To ask	sormak	sor mak
To undress	soyunmak	soy oon mak
To say	söylemek	soy leh mek
To joke	şaka yapmak	sha ka yap mak
To sing	şarkı söylemek	shar kuh soy leh mek
To comb	taramak	ta ra mak
To weigh	tartmak	tart mak
To carry	taşımak	ta shuh mak

Chapters

Learn Turkish In One Week

English	Turkish	Pronunciation
To taste	tatmak	tat mak
To repeat	tekrarlamak	tek rar la mak
To clean	temizlemek	teh meez leh mek
To thank	teşekkür etmek	tesh eh cur et mek
To have a shave	tıraş olmak	tuh rash ol mak
To climb	tırmanmak	tur man mak
To hold	tutmak	toot mak
To arrest	tutuklamak	too took la mak
To fly	uçmak	ooch mak
To forget	unutmak	oon oot mak
To wake up	uyanmak	oo yan mak
To warn	uyarmak	oo yar mak
To sleep	uyumak	oo yoo mak
To blow	üflemek	oof leh mek
To iron	ütülemek	oo too leh mek
To arrive	varmak	var mak
To hit	vurmak	voo r mak
To burn	yakmak	yak mak
To do	yapmak	yap mak

Chapters

Learn Turkish In One Week

English	Turkish	Pronunciation
To create	yaratmak	ya rat mak
To forbid	yasaklamak	ya sak la mak
To live	yaşamak	ya sha mak
To spread	yaymak	yeye mak
To write	yazmak	yaz mak
To eat	yemek	yeh mek
To defeat	yenmek	yen mek
To catch	yetişmek	yeh teesh mek
To wash	yıkamak	yuk a mak
To tear	yırtmak	yurt mak
To punch	yumruklamak	yoom rook la mak
To walk	yürümek	yoo roo mek
To swim	yüzmek	yewz mek
To force	zorlamak	zor la mak
To beg	yalvarmak	yal var mak
To lick	yalamak	yal a mak
To lie down	uzanmak	oo zan mak
To scratch	tırmalamak	tur ma la mak
To harm	zarar vermek	za rar veh mek

Chapters

Learn Turkish In One Week

English	Turkish	Pronunciation
More words	daha fazla kelime	da ha faz la keh lee meh
And	ve	veh
Or	veya	veh ya
But	ama	a ma
After	sonra	son ra
Now	şimdi	sheem dee
There is / there are	var	var
With	ile	ee leh
With the train / by train	tren ile	tren ee leh
With the car / by car	araba ile	a ra ba ee leh
This / this one	bu	boo
That / that one	o	oe
That one	şu	shoo
He / she / it	o	oe
I / myself	ben	ben
Many / much / very	çok	chok
Very good	çok iyi	chok ee
What / huh?	ne	neh
Like	gibi	gee bee

Chapters

Learn Turkish In One Week

English	Turkish	Pronunciation
Like a pig	domuz gibi	doh mooz gee bee
More	daha	da ha
Not / isn't	değil	deh eel
I am not	ben değilim	ben deh eel im
Not good	iyi değil	ee deh eel
Not well	iyi değil	ee deh eel
Every, any, each	her	her
Thing, stuff, matter	şey	shay
Everything	her şey	her shay
We	biz	beez
Job, work, business	iş	eesh
There is none	yok	yok
Unavailable	yok	yok
Large, big, massive	büyük	boo yewk
Middle	orta	or ta
A bit, a little	az	az
Very little	çok az	cok az
Open	açık	a chuk
Closed	kapalı	kap a luh

Chapters

Learn Turkish In One Week

English	Turkish	Pronunciation
Expensive	pahalı	pa ha luh
Immediately	hemen	heh men
Go immediately	hemen git	heh men geet
Hour, clock, watch	saat	sarrt
Single	tek	tek
A single one	tek bir	tek beer
Together	birlikte	beer leek teh
Family, folk, kin	aile	eye leh
Power, strength, force	güç	gewch
Powerful	güçlü	gewch loo
Perhaps	belki	bel kee
True, real, factual	gerçek	ger chek
Quite, so	pek	pek
Especially	özellikle	ur zel leek leh
If	eğer	ay er
High	yüksek	yewk sek
God	Allah	al la
Coming from	gelen	gel en
A few, some	birkaç	beer kach

Chapters

Learn Turkish In One Week

English	Turkish	Pronunciation
Question	soru	soh roo
Part, piece, bit	parça	par cha
Newspaper	gazete	gaz eh teh
Of course	tabii	ta bee
Body	vücut	voo joot
Transaction	işlem	eesh lem
Short, brief	kısa	kuh sa
Easy, simple	kolay	koh leye
Ratio, rate	oran	oe ran
Which	hangi	han gee
Soil, earth, ground	toprak	top rak
Separate, apart	ayrı	eye ruh
Price	fiyat	fee yat
Grief, sorrow	acı	a juh
Floor, storey	kat	kat
Market	pazar	pa zar
Smell	koku	koe koo
Bad	kötü	kur too
Reason, cause, motive	sebep	seb ep

Chapters

Learn Turkish In One Week

Marmaris

Marmaris is a popular tourist resort on the Mediterranean coast, located in the Muğla Province of southwestern Turkey. It relies heavily on tourism and in peak season the atmosphere is electric with bundles of things to do. Before the tourists arrived, life was quiet and peaceful in this once, small fishing village. Summer is exceptionally hot in Marmaris with temperatures constantly reaching above 40 °C in July and August

Marmaris offers luxury hotels, stunning apartments, fabulous holiday homes and awesome villas and is one of Europes most popular tourist destination on Turkey's Aegean coast.

Visit the castle and museum, take a daily boat trip, go to the old town, stroll down to the harbour and marina. There's daly tours and excursions, water parks, scuba diving, 4 x 4 off road safari, quad and buggy safari, Turkish bath or just chill on the beach. If that's not enough, there's hundreds of restaurants and some of the best nightclubs in Turkey. I can honestly guarantee a fabulous holiday in Marmaris.

Chapters

Learn Turkish In One Week

Months

English	Turkish	Pronunciation
January	Ocak	oe jak
February	Şubat	shoo bat
March	Mart	mart
April	Nisan	nee san
May	Mayıs	meye us
June	Haziran	ha zee ran
Temmuz	Temmuz	tem mooz
August	Ağustos	ow oo stoss
September	Eylül	ay lewl
October	Ekim	ay keem
November	Kasım	ka sum
December	Aralık	aa ra luk
Month	ay	eye
What month is it?	hangi aydayız	han gee eye deye uz
Month of July	temmuz ayı	tem mooz eye uh
One month	bir ay	beer eye
Two months	iki ay	ee kee eye
Year	yıl	yul
This year	bu yıl	boo yul

Chapters

Learn Turkish In One Week

Numbers

English	Turkish	Pronunciation
One	bir	beer / b ear
Two	iki	ee kee
Three	üç	ooch
Four	dört	durt
Five	beş	besh
Six	altı	al tuh
Seven	yedi	yeh dee
Eight	sekiz	seh keez
Nine	dokuz	doh kooz
Ten	on	on
Eleven	on bir	on bir
Twelve	on iki	on ee kee
Thirteen	on üç	on ooch
Fourteen	on dört	on durt
Fifteen	on beş	on besh
Sixteen	on altı	on al tuh
Seventeen	on yedi	on yeh dee
Eighteen	on sekiz	on seh keez
Nineteen	on dokuz	on doh kooz

Chapters

Learn Turkish In One Week

English	Turkish	Pronunciation
Twenty	yirmi	yeer mee
Twenty one	yirmi bir	yeer mee beer
Twenty two	yirmi iki	yeer mee ee kee
Twenty nine	yirmi dokuz	yeer mee doh kooz
Thirty	otuz	oh tooz
Forty	kırk	kurk
Fifty	elli	eh lee
Sixty	altmış	alt mush
Seventy	yetmiş	yet meesh
Eighty	seksen	sek sen
Ninety	doksan	dok san
One hundred	yüz	yewz
One hundred and one	yüz bir	yewz beer
One Thousand	bin	been
Ten thousand	on bin	on been
One hundred thousand	yüz bin	yewz been
One million	bir milyon	beer meel yee on
Ten million	on milyon	on meel yee on
One billion	bir milyar	beer meel yar

Chapters

Learn Turkish In One Week

Police

English	Turkish	Pronunciation
Police	polis	poh lee s
Police station	karakol	ka ra col
Where's the police station?	polis karakolu nerede	poh lee s ka ra col oo ner eh deh
My name is	benim adım	ben eem a dum
I'm English	ben ingiliz'im	ben een gee leez eem
Policeman	polis	poh lee s
Police woman	polis kadın	poh lee s ka dun
Watch	saat	sart
My watch was stolen	saatim çalındı	sar teem cha lun duh
Bag	çanta	chan ta
My bag was stolen	çantam çalındı	chan tam cha lun duh
Money	para	pa ra
My money was stolen	param çalındı	pa ram cha lun duh
Wallet	cüzdan	jooz dan
My wallet was stolen	cüzdanım çalındı	jooz dan um cha lun duh
Passport	pasaport	pass a port
My passport was stolen	pasaportum çalındı	pass a port oom cha lun duh
I'm innocent	ben masumum	ben ma soom oom

Chapters

Learn Turkish In One Week

Pamukkale

Pamukkale, which means "cotton castle" in Turkish is a beautiful, natural site in the Denizli province, in southwestern Turkey. People have visited this area for thousands of years due to the attraction of its thermal pools. The area is famous for a carbonate mineral left behind by the flowing of thermal spring water. In the 1960's many hotels were built to accommodate the vast number of tourist visiting this amazing site, but these have since been demolished because they were draining the thermal waters into their swimming pools which caused a lot of damage to this now protected site. It is recognised as a "World Heritage Site" and the underground volcanic activity which causes the hot springs also forced carbon dioxide into a cave, which was called the "Plutonium", which means "place of the god Pluto. The cave was used by priests for religious purposes. These priests who found ways to appear immune to the suffocating gases. There are 17 hot springs with temperatures ranging from 35 °C (95 °F) to 100 °C (212 °F). At the top of the travertine formation their is an ancient Greco- Roman city called Hierapolis. This truly is an amazing place to visit and one not to be missed.

Chapters

Learn Turkish In One Week

Pronouns

English	Turkish	Pronunciation
I	ben	ben
You	sen	sen
He / she	o	oe
We	biz	beez
You	siz	seez
They	onlar	on lar
Tired	yorgun	yor goon
I'm tired	ben yoruldum	ben yor ool doom
I'm tired (also)	ben yorgunum	ben yor goo noom
You are tired	sen yorgunsun	sen yor goon soon
He/she is tired	o yorgun	oe yor goon
We are tired	biz yorulduk	beez yor ool dook
You are tired	siz yoruldunuz	seez yor ool doon ooz
They are tired	onlar yoruldular	on lar yor ool doo lar
My	benim	ben eem
Your	senin	sen een
His / her	onun	on oon
Our	bizim	bee zeem
Your	sizin	seez een

Chapters

Learn Turkish In One Week

English	Turkish	Pronunciation
Their	onların	on lar un
Pencil	kalem	ka lem
My pencil	benim kalemim	ben eem ka lem eem
Your pencil	senin Kalemin	sen een ka lem in
His / her pencil	onun kalemi	on oon ka lem ee
This	bu	boo
These	bunlar	boo lar
This pencil is mine	bu kalem benim	boo ka lem ben eem
That	o	oe
That pencil is mine	o kalem benim	oe ka lem ben eem
This is white	bu beyaz	boo bay az
These are white	bunlar beyaz	boon lar bay az
Here	burada	boo ra da
The spoon is here	kaşık burada	ka shuk boo ra da
There	orada	or a da
The spoon is there	kaşık orada	ka shuk or a da
What	ne	neh
What did you do?	sen ne yaptın	sen neh yap tun
What do you want?	ne istiyorsun	neh ee stee yor soon

Chapters

Learn Turkish In One Week

English	Turkish	Pronunciation
What are you doing?	ne yapıyorsun	neh yap uh yor soon
Which?	hangi	han gee
Which one?	hangisi	han gee see
Which one is mine?	hangisi benim	han gee see ben eem
Which one is yours?	hangisi senin	han gee see sen een
Mine	benim	ben eem
Yours	senin	sen een
The choice is yours	seçim senin	seh cheem sen een
Who	kim	keem
Whose	kimin	keem een
Why	neden	neh den
When	ne zaman	neh za man
Everyone	herkes	her kes
Everything	her şey	her shay
Everything please	her şey lütfen	her shay lewt fen
Someone	birisi	beer ee see
Somewhere	bir yer	beer yer
Somewhere else	başka bir yer	bash ka beer yer
Something	bir şey	beer shay

Chapters

Learn Turkish In One Week

English	Turkish	Pronunciation
Something else	başka bir şey	bash ka beer shay
I want something else	başka bir şey istiyorum	bash ka birr shay is tee yor um
Do you want something else?	başka bir şey ister misin	bash ka beer shay ee ster mee seen
To me	bana	ba na
Give to me	bana ver	ba na ver
To you	sana	sa na
I give to you	sana veriyorum	sa na veh ree yor oom
From me	benden	ben den
From you	senden	sen den
From him / her	ondan	on dan
From us	bizden	beez den
From you	sizden	seez den
From them	sizden	on lar den
This is from me	bu benden	boo ben den
This is from us	bu bizden	boo beez den
Myself	kendim	ken deem
Yourself	kendin	ken deen
Himself / herself	kendi	ken dee
Ourselves	kendimiz	ken dee meez

Chapters

Learn Turkish In One Week

Restaurant

English	Turkish	Pronunciation
Waiter / waitress	garson	gar son
Hello, excuse me	pardon bakar mısınız	par don ba kar muh sun uz
Excuse me waiter	garson bey bakar mısınız	gar son bay ba kar muh sun uz
To eat	yemek	yeh mek
I don't eat red meat	kırmızı et yemiyorum	Kur muh zuh et yeh mee yor oom
I don't eat eggs	yumurta yemiyorum	yoo mur ta yeh mee yor oom
I'm vegetarian	ben vejetaryenim	ben veh shyeh tar ee en eem
To order	sipariş vermek	see pa reesh ver mek
I ordered a cake	pasta sipariş ettim	pa sta see pa reesh et teem
Cake	pasta	pa sta
I ordered pizza	pizza sipariş ettim	pee za see pa reesh et teem
Should we order pizza	pizza sipariş edelim mi	pee za see pa rish ed eh leem mee
Water	su	soo
Can I have a glass of cold water	bir bardak soğuk su alabilir miyim	bir bar dak soe ook soo a la beel ir meem
Dessert	tatlı	tat luh
Chef	şef	shef
The food was very delicious	yemekler çok lezzetliydi	yeh mek ler chok lez et lee dee
This restaurants chef is very talented	bu restoranın şefi çok yetenekli	boo res tor ran un shef ee chok yeh ten ek lee

Chapters

Learn Turkish In One Week

English	Turkish	Pronunciation
Restaurant	restoran	res tor an
Bill	hesap	heh sap
Bill please	hesap lütfen	heh sap lewt fen
Tasty	lezzetli	leh zet lee
It looks very delicious	çok lezzetli görünüyor	chok leh zet lee guh ruh nuh yor
Welcome	hoşgeldiniz	hosh gell dee neez
Do you have a reservation?	rezervasyonunuz var mı	reh zer vas yon un uz var muh
Good evening	iyi akşamlar	ee ak sham lar
Follow me please	lütfen beni takip ediniz	lewt fen ben ee ta keep eh deen iz
This way please	bu taraftan lütfen	boo ta raf tan lewt fen
Where would you like to sit?	nerede oturmak istersiniz	ner eh deh oh tur mak eester seen iz
Is there a table free	boş masa var mı	bosh ma sa var muh
Waiter?	garson bey	ga son bay
Yes sir	efendim	ef en deem
Yes sir	buyrun	boy run
Here you are	buyrun	boy run
Do you have a menu?	yemek listesi var mı	yeh mek leece teh see var muh
A menu please	yemek listesi lütfen	yeh mek leece teh see lewt fen

Chapters

Learn Turkish In One Week

English	Turkish	Pronunciation
I want	istiyorum	eestee yor oom
Do you want a drink?	içecek ister misin	eech eh jek ee ster mee sin
Do you want anything else?	başka bir şey ister misin	bash ka beer shay ee ster mee sin
No thanks	hayır teşekkürler	heye ur teh shek koo ler
Some more?	biraz daha	beer az da ha
Yes please	evet lütfen	eh vet lewt fen
Some more bread?	biraz daha ekmek	beer az da ha ek mek
Some more wine please	biraz daha şarap lütfen	beer az da ha sha rap lewt fen
Serviette	peçete	peh cheh teh
Glass	bardak	bar dak
Knife	bıçak	buh chak
Fork	çatal	cha tal
Spoon	kaşık	ka shuk
Can I have some more coffee	biraz daha kahve alabilir miyim	beer az da ha caa veh a la beel ir meem
Cheers	şerefe	sher eh feh
It was excellent	mükemmeldi	mew kem mel dee
This is very hot	bu çok sıcak	boo chok suh jak
Delicious	nefis	neh feece

Chapters

Learn Turkish In One Week

English	Turkish	Pronunciation
Good appetite	afiyet olsun	a fee yet ol sun
Enjoy your meal	afiyet olsun	a fee yet ol sun
This is very cold	bu çok soğuk	boo chok soe ook
This is overcooked	bu çok pişmiş	boo chok peesh meesh
This is undercooked	bu az pişmiş	boo az peesh meesh
This is too salty	bu çok tuzlu	boo chok tooz loo
This is too sweet	bu çok tatlı	boo choe k tat luh
This is stale	bu bayat	boo beye at
I ordered ice cream	dondurma istemiştim	don dur ma eestem eesh tim
The bill	hesap	heh sap
The bill please	hesap lütfen	heh sap lewt fen
Can I have the bill please	hesap alabilir miyim lütfen	heh sap al a beel ir meem lewt fen
Separate bills please	hesap ayrı olsun lütfen	her sap eye ruh ol sun lewt fen
The bill is too much	hesap çok fazla	heh sap chok faz la
Keep the change	üstü kalsın	oos too karl sun
Thanks for a lovely evening	güzel bir akşam için teşekkürler	goo zel beer ak sham eech in teh shek kur ler
Goodbye	güle güle	goo leh goo leh
Goodnight	iyi geceler	ee geh jel er

Chapters

Learn Turkish In One Week

School

English	Turkish	Pronunciation
School	okul	oe cool
Teacher	öğretmen	ur ret men
I'm a teacher	ben bir öğretmenim	ben beer ur ret meh neem
History	tarih	tar ee
Math	matematik	ma teh ma teek
Algebra	cebir	jeh bir
Science	fen	fen
Pen / Pencil	kalem	ka lem
Ruler	cetvel	jet vel
Paper	kağıt	kaa ut
University	üniversite	oon ee ver see teh
High school	lise	lee seh
Kindergarten	ana okulu	an a oe koo loo
Blackboard	kara tahta	ka ra tar ta
Art	sanat	san at
Backpack	sırt çantası	surt chan ta suh
Bilingual	iki dil bilen	ee kee deel bee len
Biology	biyoloji	bee yoe loh shyee
Book	kitap	kee tap

Chapters

Learn Turkish In One Week

English	Turkish	Pronunciation
Business	iş	eesh
Cafeteria	kafeterya	ka feh ter ya
Calculate	hesaplamak	heh sap la mak
Calculator	hesap makinesi	heh sap ma keen eh see
Career	kariyer	ka ree yer
Chair	sandalye	san dal yeh
Chemistry	kimya	keem ya
Class / lesson	ders	ders
Classmate	sınıf arkadaşı	sun uf ar ka da shuh
My classmate	sınıf arkadaşım	sun uf ar ka da shum
My classmate is funny	sınıf arkadaşım komik	sun uf ar ka da shum kom eek
Classroom	sınıf	sun uf
College	kolej	kol esh
Computer	bilgisayar	beel gee sa yar
Computer science	bilgisayar bilimi	beel gee sa yar bee lee mee
Copier	fotokopi makinesi	foe toe koh pee ma keen eh see
Database	veritabanı	veh ree ta ban uh
Data	veri	veh ree
Deadline / the last day	son gün	son gewn

Chapters

Learn Turkish In One Week

English	Turkish	Pronunciation
Degree	lisans	lee sans
Desk	masa	ma sa
Dictionary	sözlük	surz lewk
Document	belge	bel geh
Economics	ekonomi	eh koh nom ee
Education	eğitim	ay teem
Employee	işçi	eesh chee
Employer	işveren	eesh veh ren
Employment	iş	eesh
Eraser	silgi	seel gee
Exam	sınav	suh nav
English	ingilizce	een gee leez jeh
Turkish	türkçe	turk cheh
Turkish	türk	turk
Geography	coğrafya	joe raf ya
Homework	ödev	ur dev
Calendar	takvim	tak veem
Language	dil	deel
Pencil sharpener	kalemtraş	ka lem trash

Chapters

Learn Turkish In One Week

Ölüdeniz

A fabulous beach resort in the Fethiye district of Muğla Province on the Turquoise Coast of southwestern Turkey. The beach is a pebble beach but it has a sandy bay at the mouth of Ölüdeniz, on the blue lagoon. The blue lagoon is a nature reserve that is protected and building or construction is strictly prohibited. The sea at Ölüdeniz is a beautiful shade of blue, turquoise and aquamarine. Those of you who struggle getting into the water will have no problems here. Two steps down and the water is past your waste and before you realise it a wave has covered the remaining parts of your body. One of Turkey's finest beach resorts.Away from the beach you'll find wonderful bars, restaurants and plenty of shops so you'll never tire of something to do.Pull up a chair, have a soft drink or a beer and sit back and watch the hundreds of tourists and professionals paragliding from Babadağ mountain. Ölüdeniz is famous for its paragliding and is regarded as one of the best places in the world to try this scary sport. If you manage the terrifying trip up Babadağ mountain then actually running off the cliff to paraglide is not all that bad and the views are breathtaking. People from all over the world come here just to take part in this exhilarating sport. Be careful walking along the promenade though, because there are different designated landing areas and at least one paraglider landing every 30 seconds.Ölüdeniz is one of my favourite places and a fun, filled adventure for everyone.

Chapters

Learn Turkish In One Week

Time

English	Turkish	Pronunciation
What time is it	saat kaç	sart cach
It's one o'clock	saat bir	sart bir
It's two o'clock	saat iki	sart ee kee
It's eleven o'clock	saat on bir	sart on bir
It's exactly five o'clock	saat tam olarak beş	sart tam oh la rack besh
It's exactly eight o'clock	saat tam olarak sekiz	sart tam oh la rack seh keez
It's half past three	Saat üç buçuk	sart ooch boo chook
It's five past one	biri beş geçiyor	bir ree besh gech ee yor
It's twenty past four	dördü yirmi geçiyor	dur dew yir me gech ee yor
It's quarter past seven	yediyi çeyrek geçiyor	yedee ee cheh rek gech ee yor
It's five to three	üçe beş var	ooch eh besh var
It's quarter to nine	dokuza çeyrek var	dock koo za cheye rek var
Is this clock right	bu saat doğru mu	boo sart doe roo moo
You're early today	bugün erkencisin	boo gewn er ken ji seen
You're late	geç kaldınız	gech cal dun uz
I'm sorry I'm late	özür dilerim geciktim	ur zur dee leh reem geh jick tim
It's too early	çok erken	chok er ken
It's too late	çok geç	chok gech
Late	geç	gech

Chapters

Learn Turkish In One Week

English	Turkish	Pronunciation
Early	erken	er ken
Morning	sabah	sa ba
In the morning	sabahleyin	sa ba lay een
Tomorrow	yarın	ya run
Tomorrow morning	yarın sabah	ya run sa ba
Night	gece	geh jeh
At night	geceleyin	geh jeh lay een
Evening	akşam	ak sham
In the evening	akşamleyin	ak sham lay een
Day	gün	gewn
Every day	her gün	her gewn
Midnight	gece yarısı	geh jeh ya ruh suh
At midnight	gece yarısında	geh jeh ya ruh sun da
Today	bugün	boo gewn
Yesterday	dün	doon
Day before yesterday	evvelsi gün	ev vel see gewn
Day after tomorrow	öbür gün	ur bur gewn
This morning	bu sabah	boo sa ba
Tonight	bu gece	boo geh jeh

Chapters

Learn Turkish In One Week

English	Turkish	Pronunciation
Yesterday morning	dün sabah	doon sa ba
Yesterday evening	dün akşam	doon ak sham
Last night	dün gece	doon geh jeh
Week	hafta	haf ta
Last week	geçen hafta	geh chen haf ta
A week ago	bir hafta önce	bir haf ta urn jeh
Month	ay	eye
Last month	geçen ay	geh chen eye
A month ago	bir ay önce	bir eye urn jeh
Year	yıl	yull
Last year	geçen yıl	geh chen yull
A year ago	bir yıl önce	bir yull urn jeh
Tomorrow evening	yarın akşam	ya run ak sham
Tomorrow night	yarın gece	ya run geh jeh
Minute	dakika	da kee ka
In one minute	bir dakika içinde	bir da kee ka eech een deh
In two minutes	iki dakika içinde	eekee da kee ka eech een deh
In ten minutes	on dakika içinde	on da kee ka eech een deh
A minute ago	bir dakika önce	bir da kee ka urn jeh

Chapters

Learn Turkish In One Week

English	Turkish	Pronunciation
Hour	saat	sart
In one hours	bir saat içinde	bir sart eech een deh
In three hours	üç saat içinde	ooch sart eech een deh
An hour ago	bir saat önce	bir sart urn jeh
Next week	gelecek hafta	gel eh jeck haf ta
Next month	gelecek ay	gel eh jeck eye
Next year	gelecek yıl	gel eh jeck yull
Daily	günlük	gewn lewk
Weekly	haftalık	haf ta luck
Monthly	aylık	eye luck
Yearly	yıllık	yull luck
Every day	her gün	her gewn
Every week	her hafta	her haf ta
Every month	her ay	her eye
Every year	her yıl	her yull
Now	şimdi	sheem dee
Soon	yakında	ya kun da
In three days	üç gün içinde	ooch gewn eech een deh
In a week	bir hafta içinde	bir haf ta eech een deh

Chapters

Learn Turkish In One Week

Weather

English	Turkish	Pronunciation
Sun	güneş	gewn esh
Sunny	güneşli	gewn esh lee
It is sunny today	bugün güneşli	boo gewn gewn esh lee
Cloud	bulut	boo loot
Cloudy	bulutlu	boo loot loo
It is very cloudy today	bugün çok bulutlu	boo gewn chok boo loot loo
Gale	bora	bor a
Ice	buz	booz
Icy	buzlu	booz loo
Weather	hava	ha va
The weather is icy	hava buzlu	ha va booz loo
Degree	derece	deh reh jeh
Temperature	sıcaklık	suh jak luk
What's the temperature today?	bugün hava kaç derece	boo gewn ha va kach deh reh jeh
Hail	dolu	doh loo
Weather forecast	hava durumu	hav a dur oo moo
Umbrella	şemsiye	shem see yeh
Raincoat	yağmurluk	yar mur look

Chapters

Learn Turkish In One Week

English	Turkish	Pronunciation
Winter	kış	kush
Spring	ilkbahar	eelk ba har
Summer	yaz	yaz
Autumn	sonbahar	son ba har
Frost	don	don
Storm	fırtına	fur tun a
Wind	rüzgar	rooz gar
Windy	rüzgarlı	rooz gar luh
Windy and cloudy	rüzgarlı ve bulutlu	rooz gar luh veh boo loot loo
Snow	kar	kar
Snow storm	kar fırtınası	kar fur tun a suh
Rain	yağmur	yar mur
Rainy	yağmurlu	yar mur loo
Rainbow	gökkuşağı	gurk koo shaa uh
How's the weather today?	bugün hava nasıl	boo gewn hav a na sul
The weather is nice	hava güzel	ha va goo zell
The weather is bad	hava kötü	ha va kur too
Cold	soğuk	soe ook
It's cold	soğuk	soe ook

Chapters

Learn Turkish In One Week

English	Turkish	Pronunciation
Hot	sıcak	suh jak
It's hot	sıcak	suh jak
It's very hot	çok sıcak	chok suh jak
Thunder	gök gürültüsü	gurk goo rool too soo
Lightning	şimşek	sheem shek
Sunset	gün batımı	gewn bat uh muh
Thunderstorm	fırtına	fur tun a
What's the weather like?	hava nasıl	hav a na sull
Is it going to rain?	yağmur yağacak mı	yaa mur yaa a jak muh
Is it going to rain today?	bugün yağmur yağacak mı	boo gewn yaa mur yaa a jak muh
The weather is hot	hava sıcak	hav a suh jak
The weather is freezing	hava buz gibi	hav a booz gee bee
The weather will be hot tomorrow	yarın hava sıcak olacak	ya run hav a suh jak ol a jak
Snowy	karlı	kar luh
The weather was cold yesterday	dün hava soğuktu	doon hav a soe ook too
It might rain	yağmur yağabilir	yaa mur yaa a bee leer
It might rain today	bugün yağmur yağabilir	boo gewn yaa mur yaa a bee leer

Chapters

Learn Turkish In One Week

Work

English	Turkish	Pronunciation
Chef	şef	shef
Actor	aktör	ack tur
Actress	aktris	ack treece
Archaeologist	arkeolog	ar keh og log
Soldier	asker	ass ker
Lawyer	avukat	a voo cat
Grocer	bakkal	bak cal
Fisherman	balıkçı	ba luk chuh
Banker	bankacı	ban ka juh
Barber	berber	ber ber
Scientist	bilim adamı	bee leem a dam uh
Glazier	camcı	jam juh
Surgeon	cerrah	jer rah
Florist	çiçekçi	chee chek chee
Farmer	çiftçi	cheeft chee
Locksmith	çilingir	chee leen gir
Shepherd	çoban	choe ban
Dancer	dansçı	dans chuh
Decorator	dekoratör	deh kor a tur

Chapters

Learn Turkish In One Week

English	Turkish	Pronunciation
Sailor	denizci	deh neez jee
Dentist	diş doktoru	deesh dok tuh roo
Doctor	doktor	dok tor
Barman	barmen	bar men
Cook	ahçı	aa chuh
Pharmacist	eczacı	edge zar juh
Electrician	elektrikçi	eh lek treek chee
Retired	emekli	eh mek lee
Real estate agent	emlakçı	em lak chuh
House wife	ev hanımı	ev han uh muh
Baker	fırıncı	fuh run juh
Film star	film yıldızı	feelm yull duh zuh
Photographer	fotoğrafçı	foh toe raf chuh
Waiter	garson	gar son
Waitress	garson	gar son
Newsagent	gazete bayii	ga zeh teh beye yee
Journalist	gazeteci	ga zeh teh jee
Customs officer	gümrük memuru	gewm rewk mem oo roo
Judge	hakim	ha keem

Chapters

Learn Turkish In One Week

English	Turkish	Pronunciation
Porter	hamal	ha mal
Nurse	hemşire	hem shee reh
Sculptor	heykeltıraş	hay kel tur ash
Stewardess	hostes	hos tes
Businessman	işadamı	eesh a dam uh
Worker	işçi	eesh chee
Fireman	itfaiyeci	eet feye yeh jee
Jockey	jokey	joe kee
Lorry driver	kamyon şoförü	cam yon show fur roo
Captain	kaptan	kap tan
Butcher	kasap	ka sap
Cashier	kasiyer	ka see yer
Hairdresser	kuaför	koo a fur
Librarian	kütüphaneci	koo toop han eh jee
Miner	madenci	mad en jee
Greengrocer	manav	man av
Model	manken	man ken
Carpenter	marangoz	ma ran goz
Printer	matbaacı	mat ba ah juh

Chapters

Learn Turkish In One Week

English	Turkish	Pronunciation
Architect	mimar	mee mar
Fashion designer	modacı	mod a juh
Reporter	muhabir	moo ha bir
Accountant	muhasebeci	moo ha seh beh jee
Inspector	müfettiş	moo feh teesh
Engineer	mühendis	moo hen dees
Builder	inşaatçı	een shart chuh
Builder	müteahhit	moo teh a heet
Musician	müzisyen	mooz ees yen
Teacher	öğretmen	ur ret men
Priest	papaz	pa paz
Pilot	pilot	pee lot
Policeman	polis	poh leece
Policewoman	kadın polis	ka dun poh leece
Politician	politikacı	poh lee tee ka juh
Postman	postacı	post a juh
Psychologist	psikolog	pee see koh log
Receptionist	resepsiyoncu	reh sep see yon joo
Artist	ressam	reh sam

Chapters

Learn Turkish In One Week

English	Turkish	Pronunciation
Prosecutor	savcı	sav juh
Secretary	sekreter	sek reh ter
Insurer	sigortacı	see gor ta juh
Plumber	su tesisatçısı	soo teh see sat chuh suh
Singer	şarkıcı	shark uh juh
Driver	şoför	show fur
Mechanic	tamirci	ta meer jee
Technician	teknisyen	tek neece yen
Interpreter	tercüman	ter joo man
Tailor	terzi	ter zee
Shop assistant	tezgâhtar	tez gar tar
Veterinary	veteriner	vet er een er
Treasurer	veznedar	vez neh dar
Publisher	yayımcı	yay um juh
Author	yazar	yaz ar
Programmer	programcı	proe gram juh
Trade unionist	sendikacı	sen dee ka juh
Sportswoman	sporcu bayan	spor joo beye an
Sportsman	sporcu erkek	spor joo er kek

Chapters

Learn Turkish In One Week

Vegetables

English	Turkish	Pronunciation
Vegetables	sebzeler	seb zell er
Peas	bezelye	bez eh lee yeh
Pepper	biber	bee ber
Tomatoe	domates	doe ma tes
Carrot	havuç	hav ooch
Spinach	ıspanak	uh span ack
Cauliflower	karnabahar	karn a ba har
Asparagus	kuşkonmaz	koosh kon maz
Cabbage	lahana	la han a
Lettuce	marul	ma rool
Lentil	mercimek	mer jee mek
Corn	mısır	muh sur
Beetroot	pancar kökü	pan jar kur kew
Potato	patates	pa ta tes
Aubergine	patlıcan	pat luh jan
Cucumber	salatalık	sal at a luk
Garlic	sarımsak	sar um sack
Cress	tere	teh reh
Radish	turp	turp

Chapters

Learn Turkish In One Week

English	Turkish	Pronunciation
Do you want vegetables	sebze ister misin	seb zeh eester mee sin
I want carrots please	havuç istiyorum lütfen	hav ooch eestee yor oom lewt fen
Apricot	kayısı	keye uh suh
Three dried apricots	üç kuru kayısı	ooch koo roo keye uh suh
Celery	kereviz	ker eh veez
Onion	soğan	soe an
Sweet potato	tatlı patates	tat luh pa ta tes
I don't like celery	kereviz sevmiyorum	ker eh veez sev mee yor oom
Carrots and potatoes	havuç ve patates	hav ooch veh pa ta tes
Eggplant	patlıcan	pat luh jan
Broccoli	brokoli	broh koh lee
One more please	bir tane daha, lütfen	bir tar neh da ha lewt fen
More carrots please	daha havuç lütfen	da ha hav ooch lewt fen
I want more please	daha istiyorum lütfen	da ha ees tee yor oom lewt fen
Lots please	çok lütfen	chok lewt fen
Just cabbage	sadece lahana	sar deh jeh la ha na
Carrots or broccoli	havuç veya brokoli	hav ooch veh ya broh koh lee
Potatoes and cabbage	patates ve lahana	pa ta tes veh la han a
Yummy / Delicious	nefis	neh feece

Chapters

Learn Turkish In One Week

Secret Bonus Page - Full Conversation

English	Turkish	Pronunciation
Hello, good morning	merhaba günaydın	mer ha ba gewn eye dun
Hello my friend	merhaba arkadaşım	mer ha ba ar ka da shum
How are you this morning	bu sabah nasılsın	boo sa ba na sull sun
I'm very good thanks	çok iyiyim teşekkürler	chok eem teh sheh kur ler
And you	ya sen	ya sen
How are you today	bugün nasılsın	boo gewn na sull sun
So so	şöyle böyle	shoy leh boy leh
The weather is beautiful today	bugün hava çok güzel	boo gewn ha va chok goo zell
Yes it is very hot	evet çok sıcak	eh vet chok suh jak
How is your mum?	annen nasıl	an nen na sool
She is good	o iyi	oe ee
And your dad?	ve senin baban	veh sen een ba ban
Not bad	fena değil	feh na deh eel
How's your sister	kızkardeşin nasıl	kuz kar desh een na sul
Not so good	pek iyi değil	pek ee deh eel
Why?	neden	neh den
She has a headache	başı ağrıyor	bash uh aa ree yor
I hope she gets over it soon	umarım yakında iyileşir	um arum ya kun da ee leh shir

Chapters

Learn Turkish In One Week

English	Turkish	Pronunciation
Thank you	teşekkür ederim	teh sheh kur eh deh reem
What are you doing today?	bugün ne yapıyorsun	boo gewn neh yap uh yor soon
I'm going to Fethiye	ben fethiye gidiyorum	ben fet ee yeh geed ee yor oom
I want a new shirt	yeni bir gömlek istiyorum	yen ee bir gurm lek ees tee yor oom
For work?	iş için	eesh eech in
No	hayır	heye ur
For Saturday	cumartesi için	joo mar teh see eech in
New girlfriend?	yeni kız arkadaş	yen ee cuz ar ka dash
Yes	evet	eh vet
Is she beautiful	o güzel mi	oe goo zel mee
Yes very beautiful	evet çok güzel	eh vet chok goo zel
What's her name?	onun adı ne	on oon a duh neh
Banu	banu	ba noo
Lovely	güzel	goo zel
Have a nice day my friend	iyi günler arkadaşım	ee goon ler ar ka da shum
See you later	sonra görüşürüz	son ra guh ruh shur uz
Goodbye	güle güle	goo leh goo leh
Goodbye	hoşça kal	hosh chak al

Chapters

Summary

Turkey is a beautiful country with warm, friendly people and once you visit this amazing country I guarantee you will return.

One week after reading this book you will be able to communicate and speak Turkish in many different situations. The important thing to remember is to practice frequently. It's not enough to say the words in your head, you have to speak them out loud. The more you practice the better you'll become.

Not many foreign people try to speak Turkish so even a few words or sentences when you are in Turkey will have the locals amazed, impressed and very appreciative. You will be looked after better and respected. Turkish people are delighted when you try to speak their language and you'll be amazed at their reaction.

Taking off from Babadağ mountain. If you're not brave enough to try this sport then just drive up the mountain, or take the cable car. Take a seat at the wonderful Turkish restaurant and watch all the other crazy people running off a cliff. You need nerves of steel though! Although the drive is a little terrifying, the views at the top are all worth while and you won't be disappointed.

I hope you enjoy this book and refer to it time and time again to improve your Turkish language skills. I also hope my passion for Turkey has rubbed off on you. It truly is one of the most amazing countries in the world.

Geoff Jackson

June 2021

Made in the USA
Monee, IL
18 October 2023

44657193R00116